FOLKLÓRICO DRESS COLORING BOOK

BY K.B. STONE

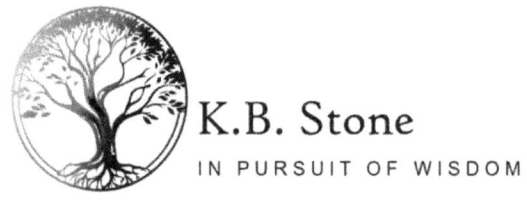

K.B. Stone
IN PURSUIT OF WISDOM

Enjoy your journey!
Disfruta tu viaje!

Intentionally Blank
Intencionalmente Blanco

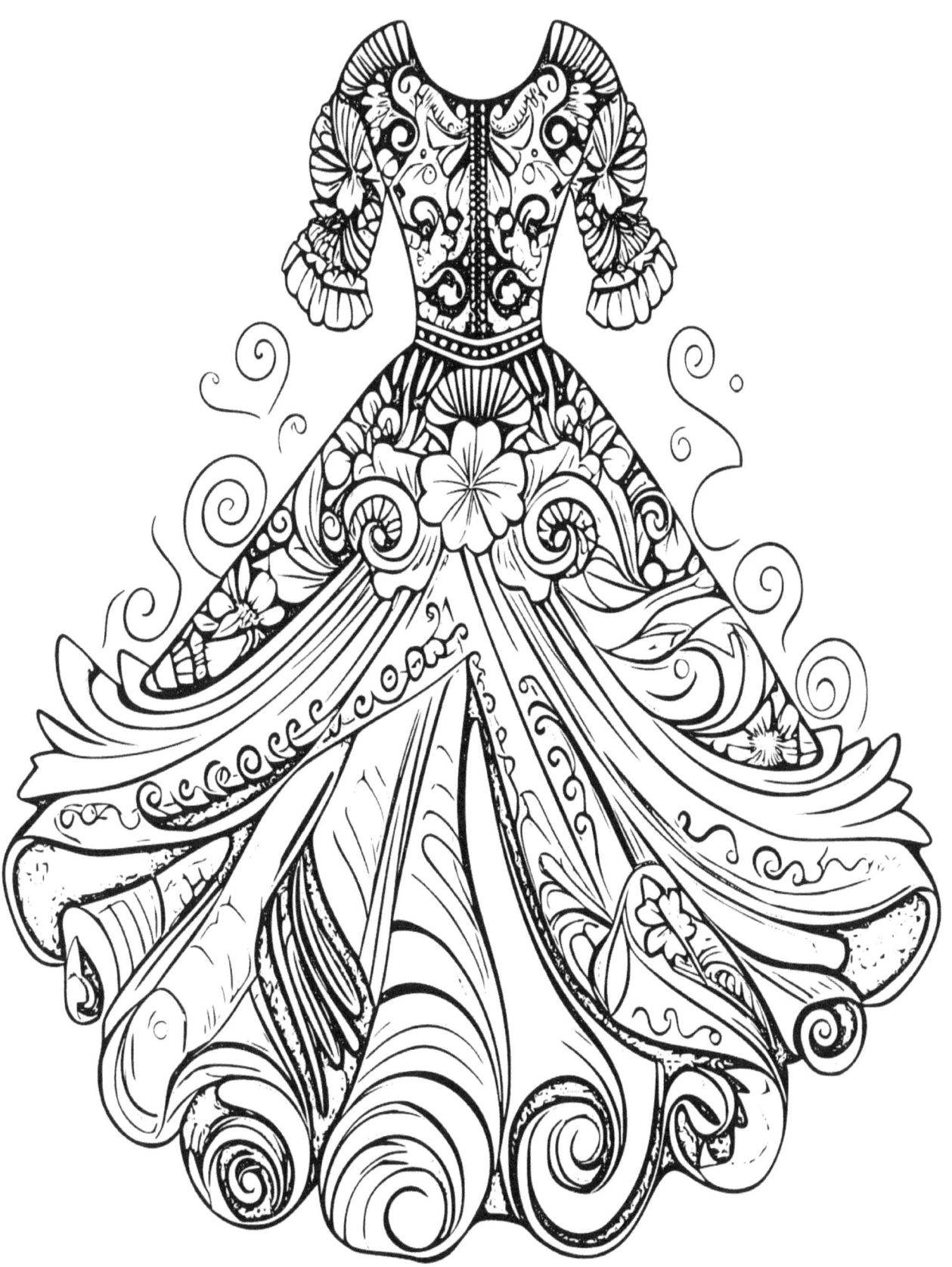

Intentionally Blank
Intencionalmente Blanco

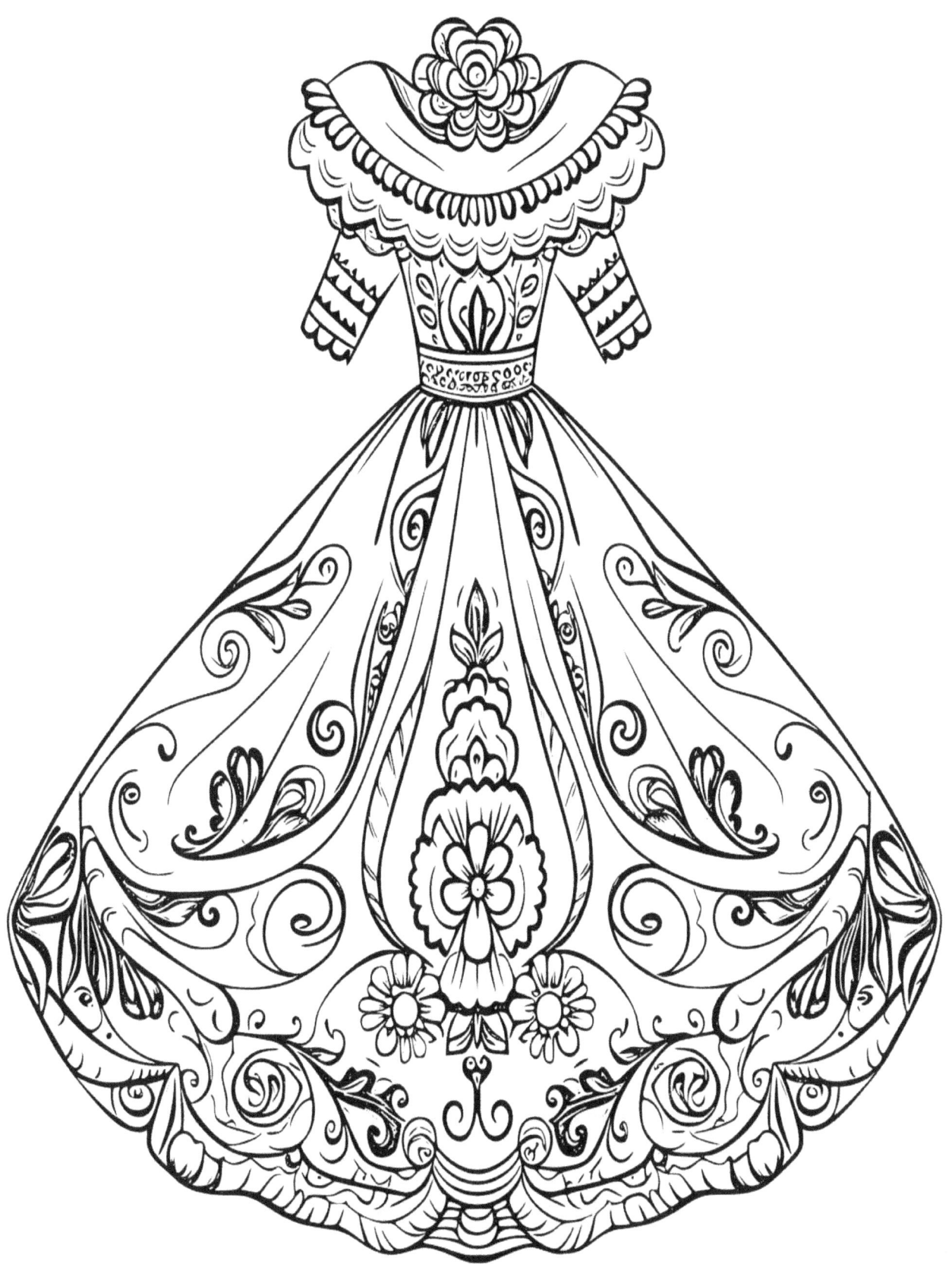

Intentionally Blank
Intencionalmente Blanco

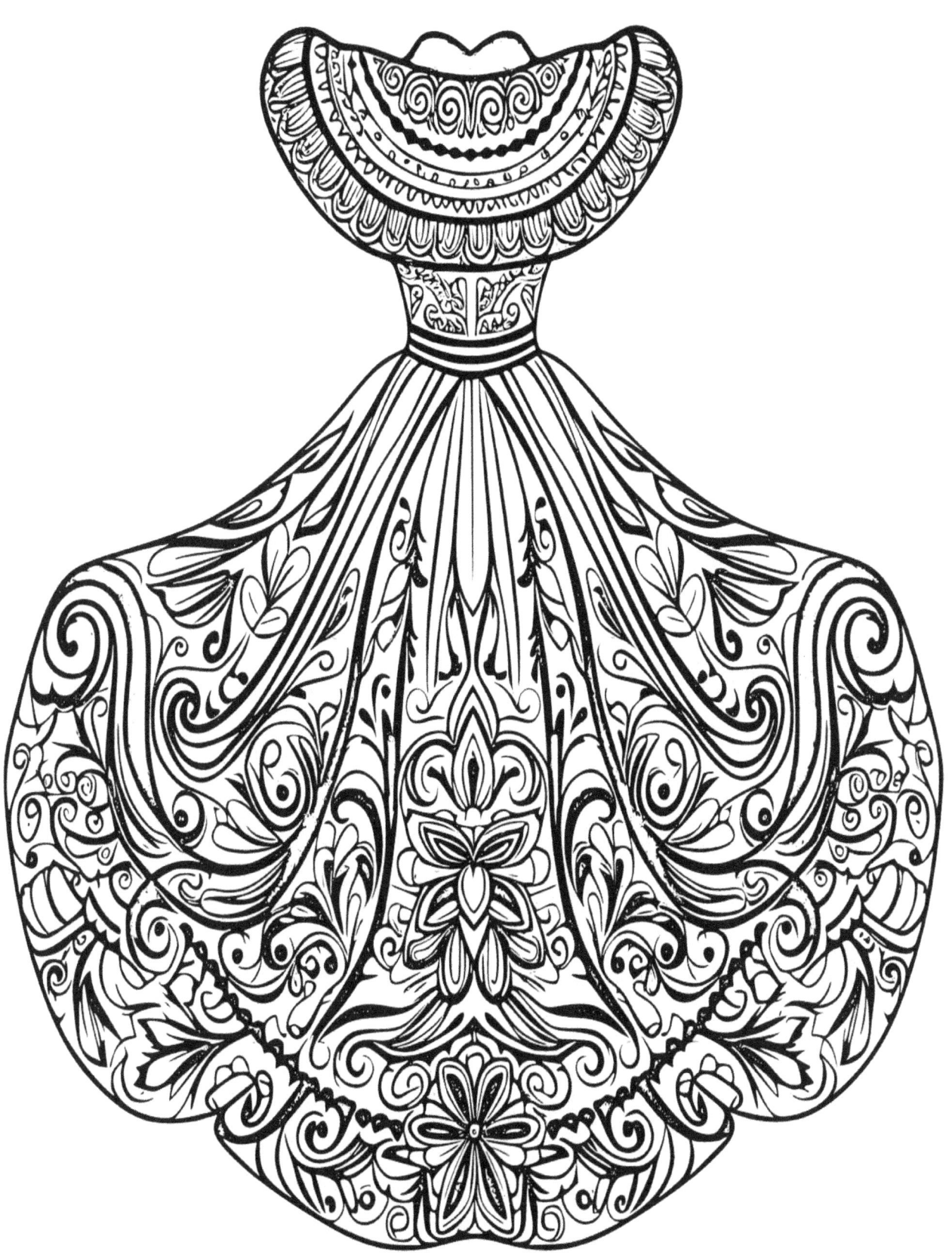

Intentionally Blank
Intencionalmente Blanco

Intentionally Blank
Intencionalmente Blanco

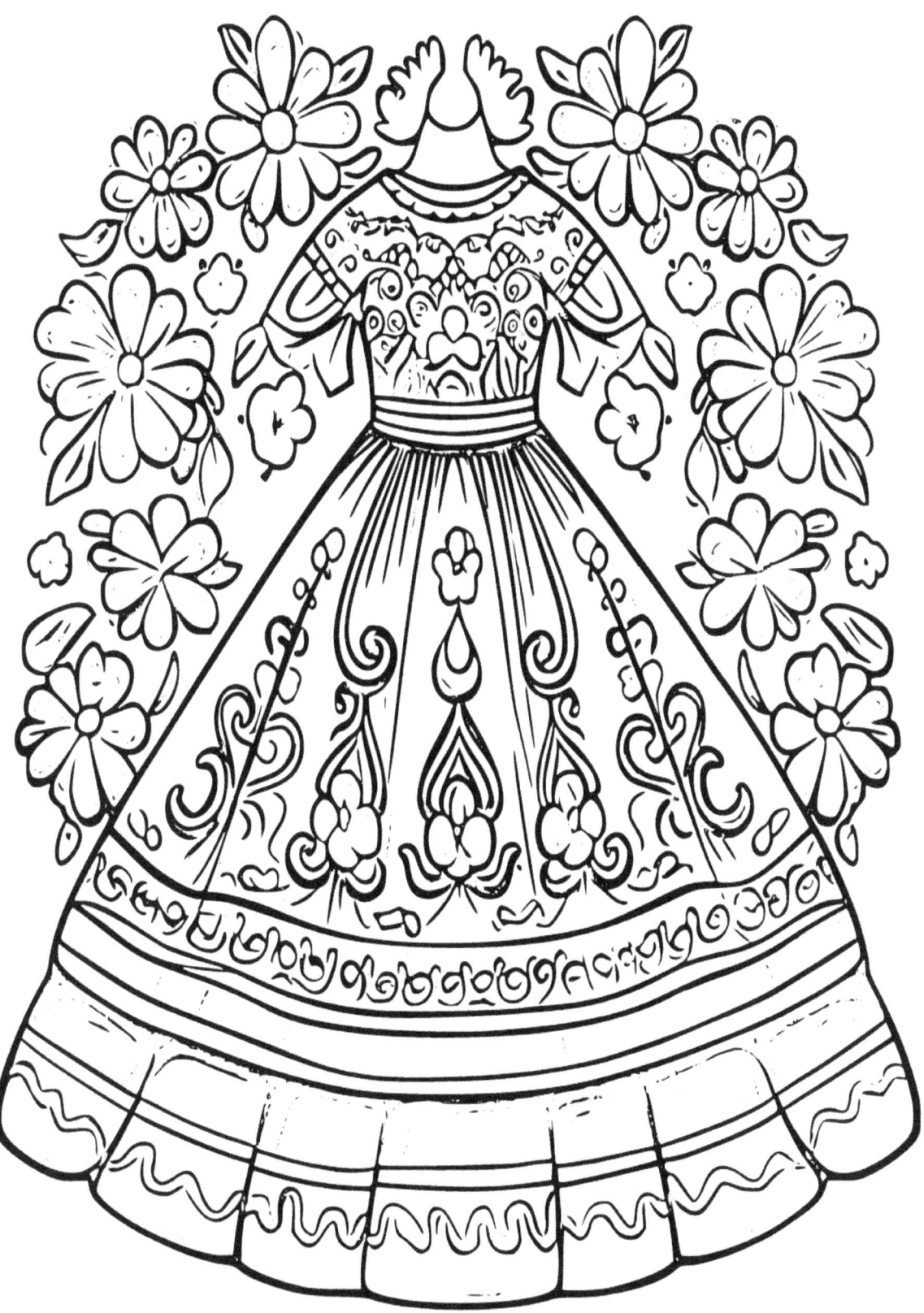

Intentionally Blank
Intencionalmente Blanco

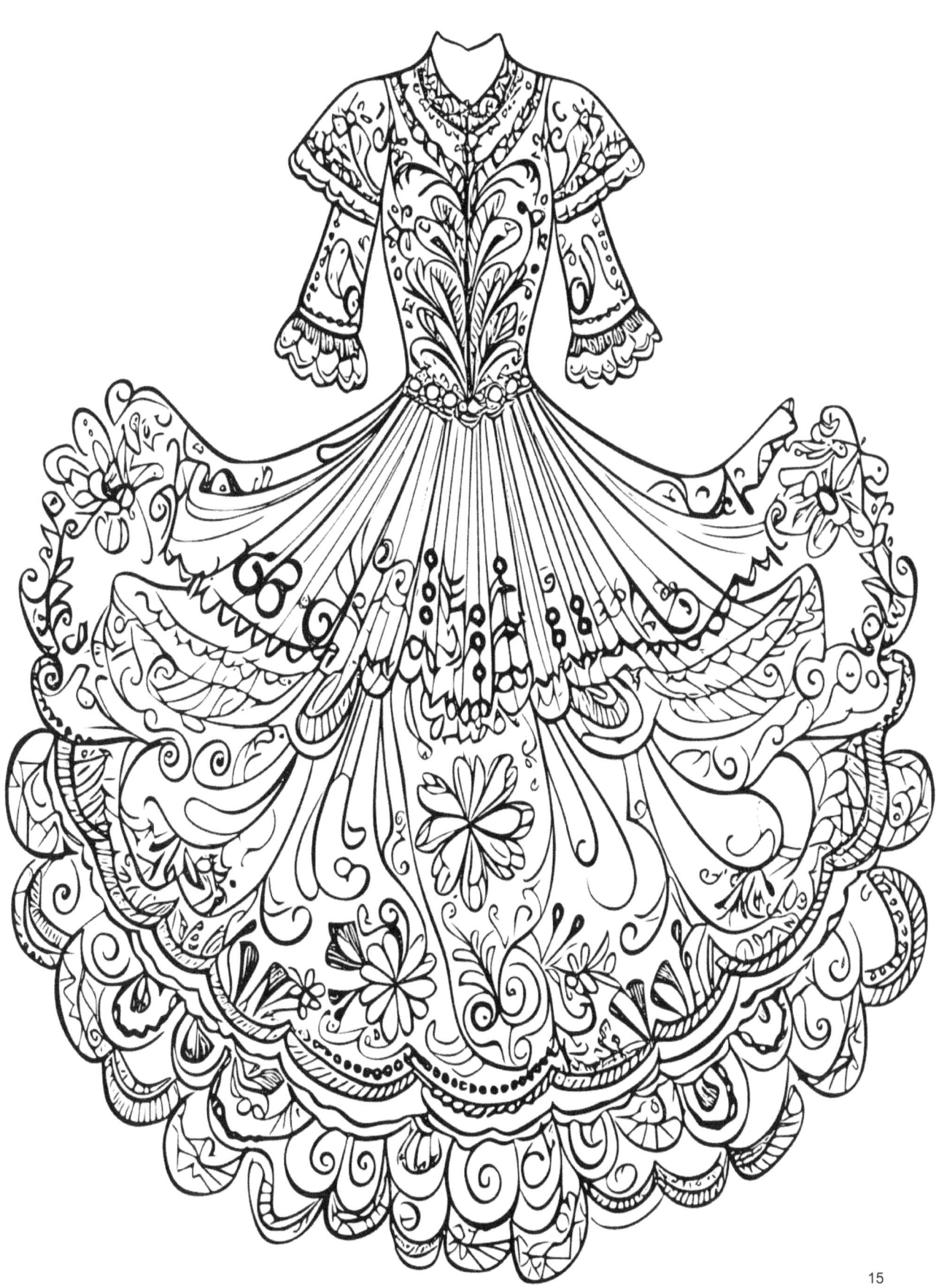

Intentionally Blank
Intencionalmente Blanco

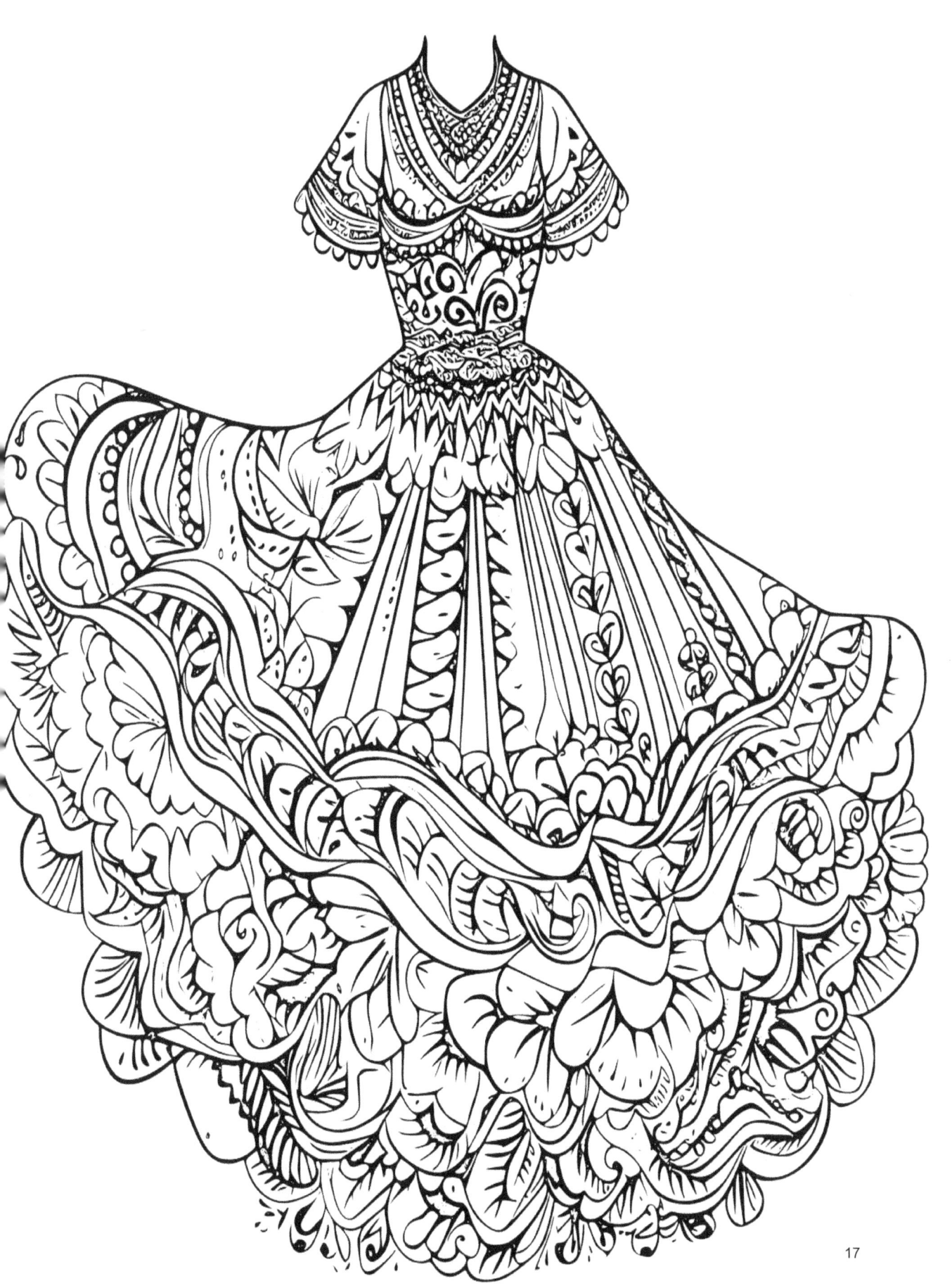

Intentionally Blank
Intencionalmente Blanco

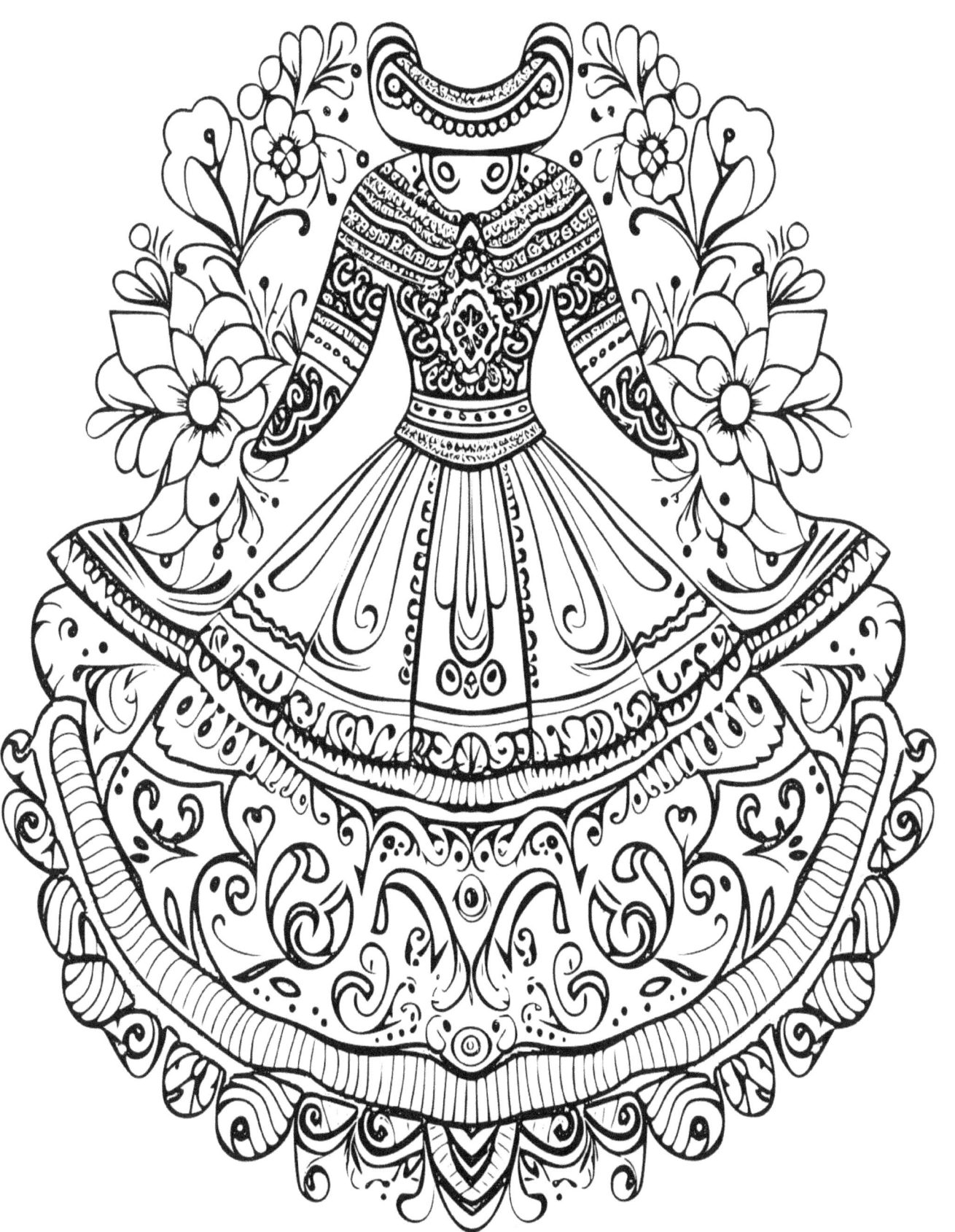

Intentionally Blank
Intencionalmente Blanco

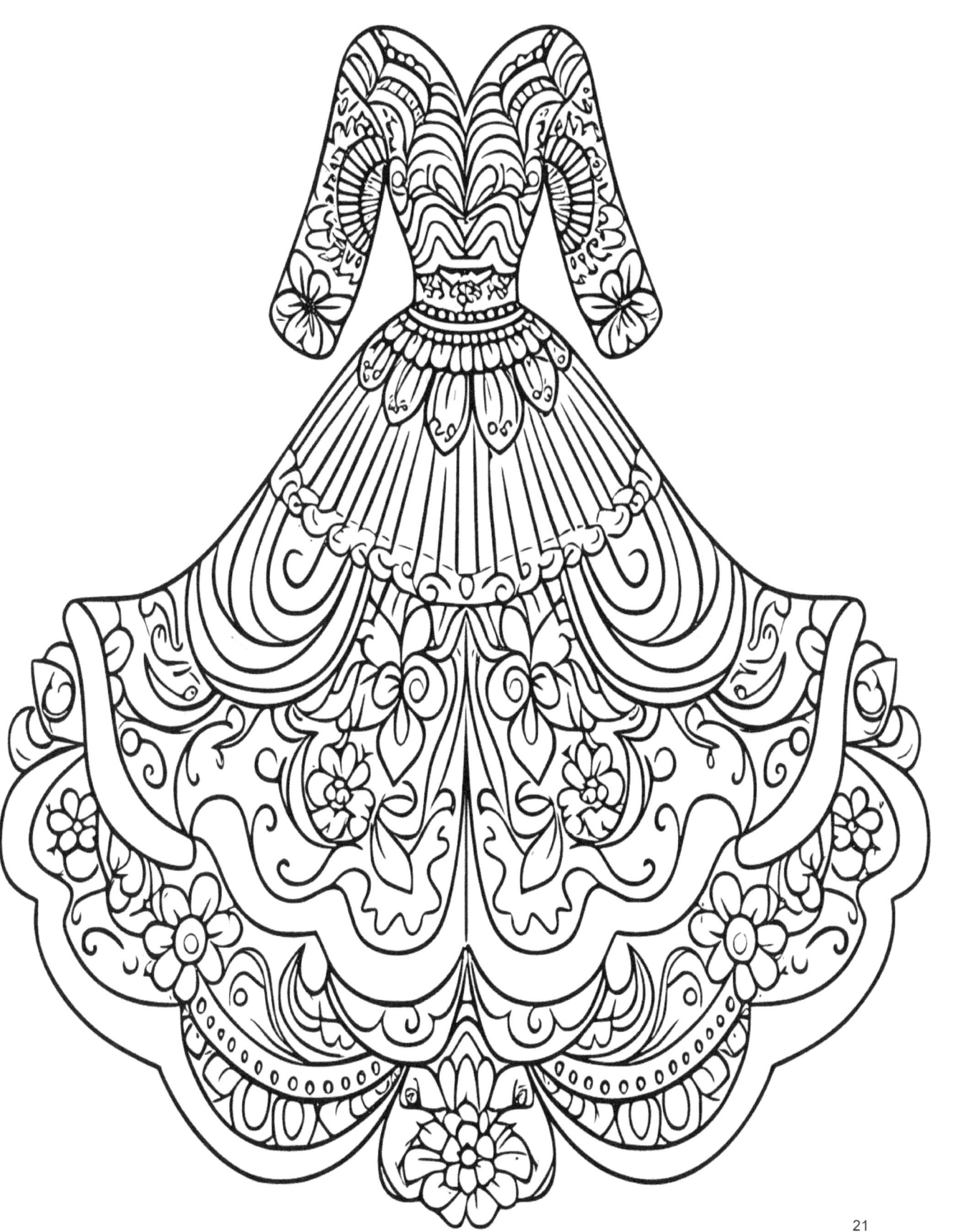

Intentionally Blank
Intencionalmente Blanco

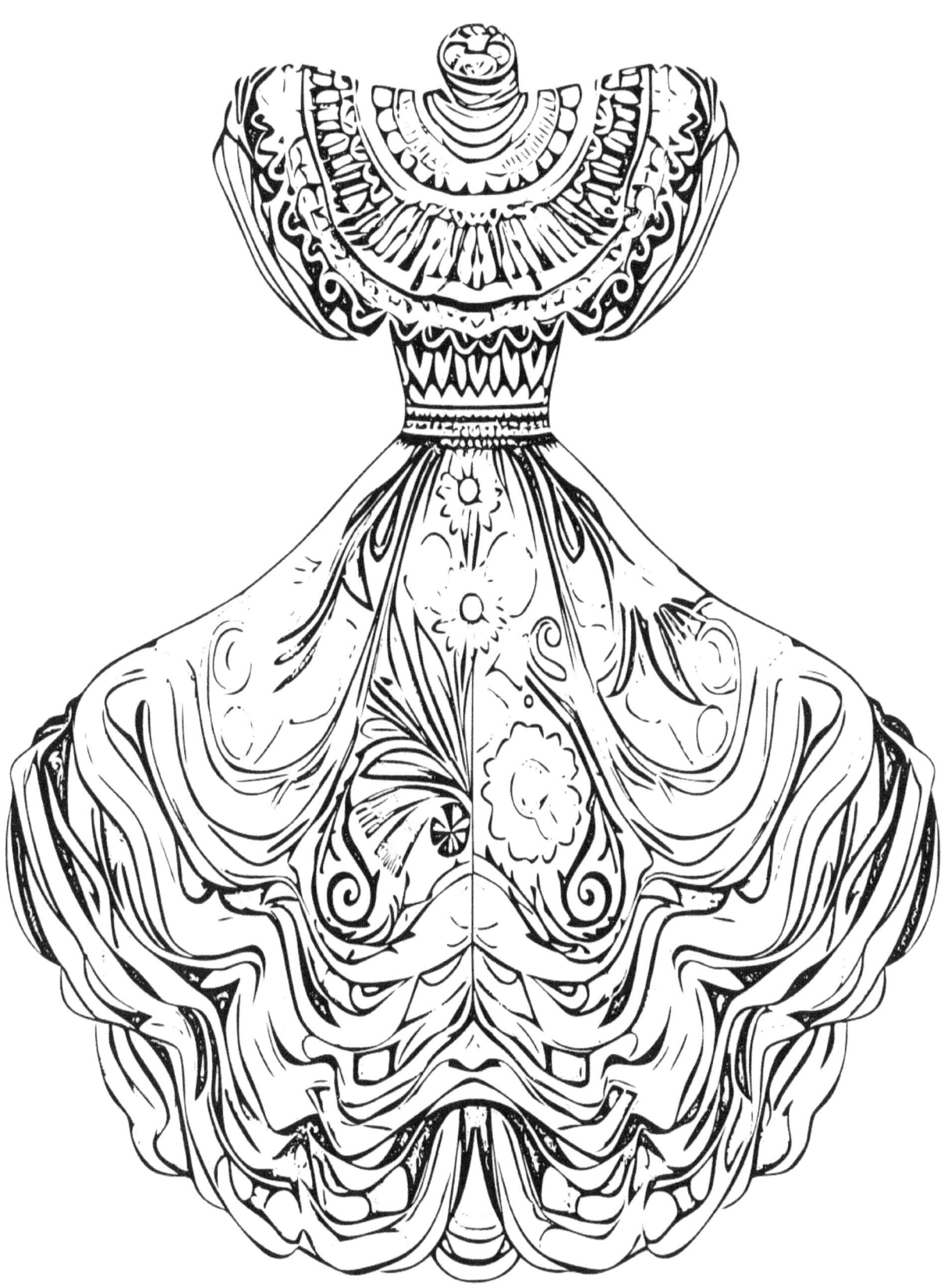

Intentionally Blank
Intencionalmente Blanco

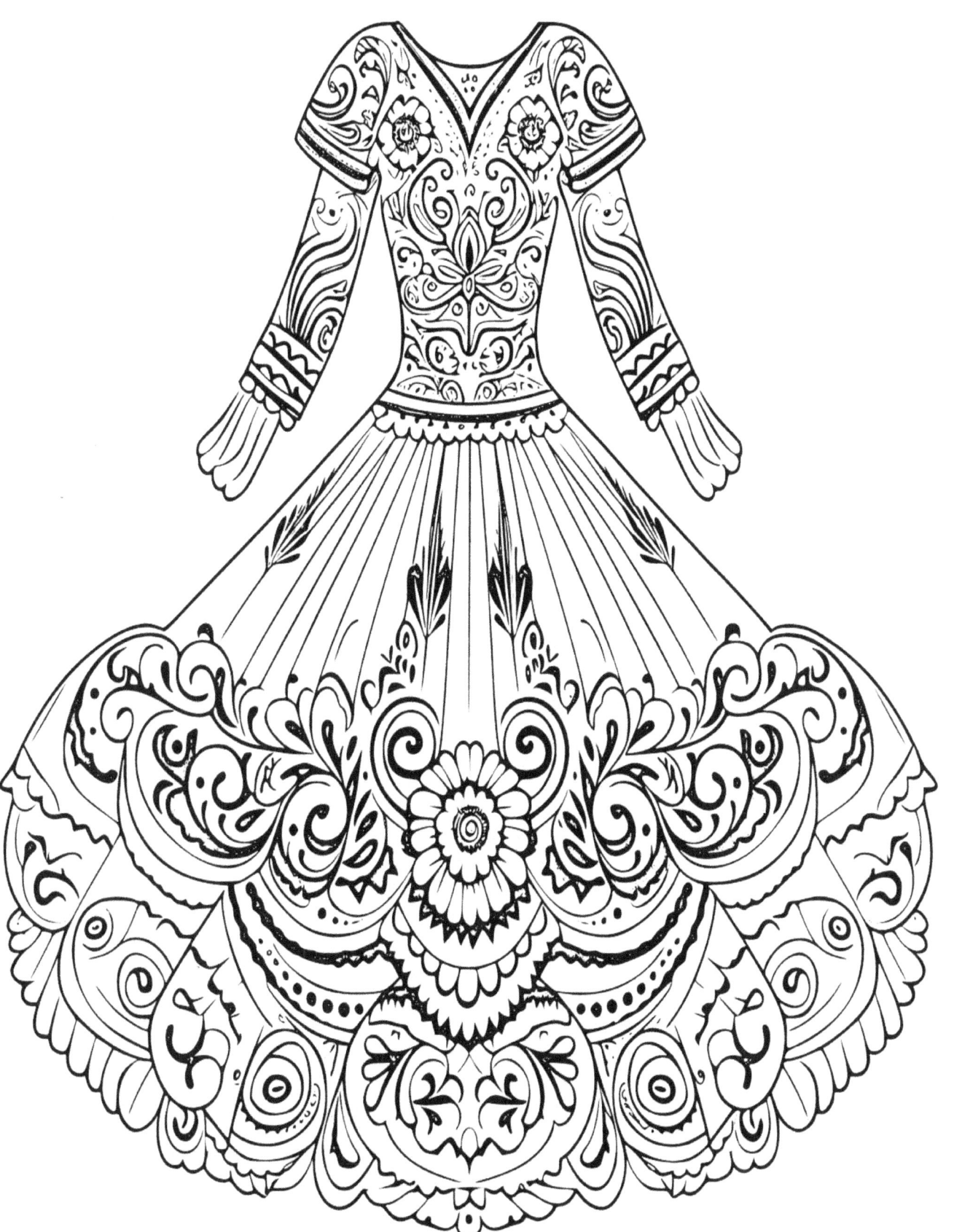

Intentionally Blank
Intencionalmente Blanco

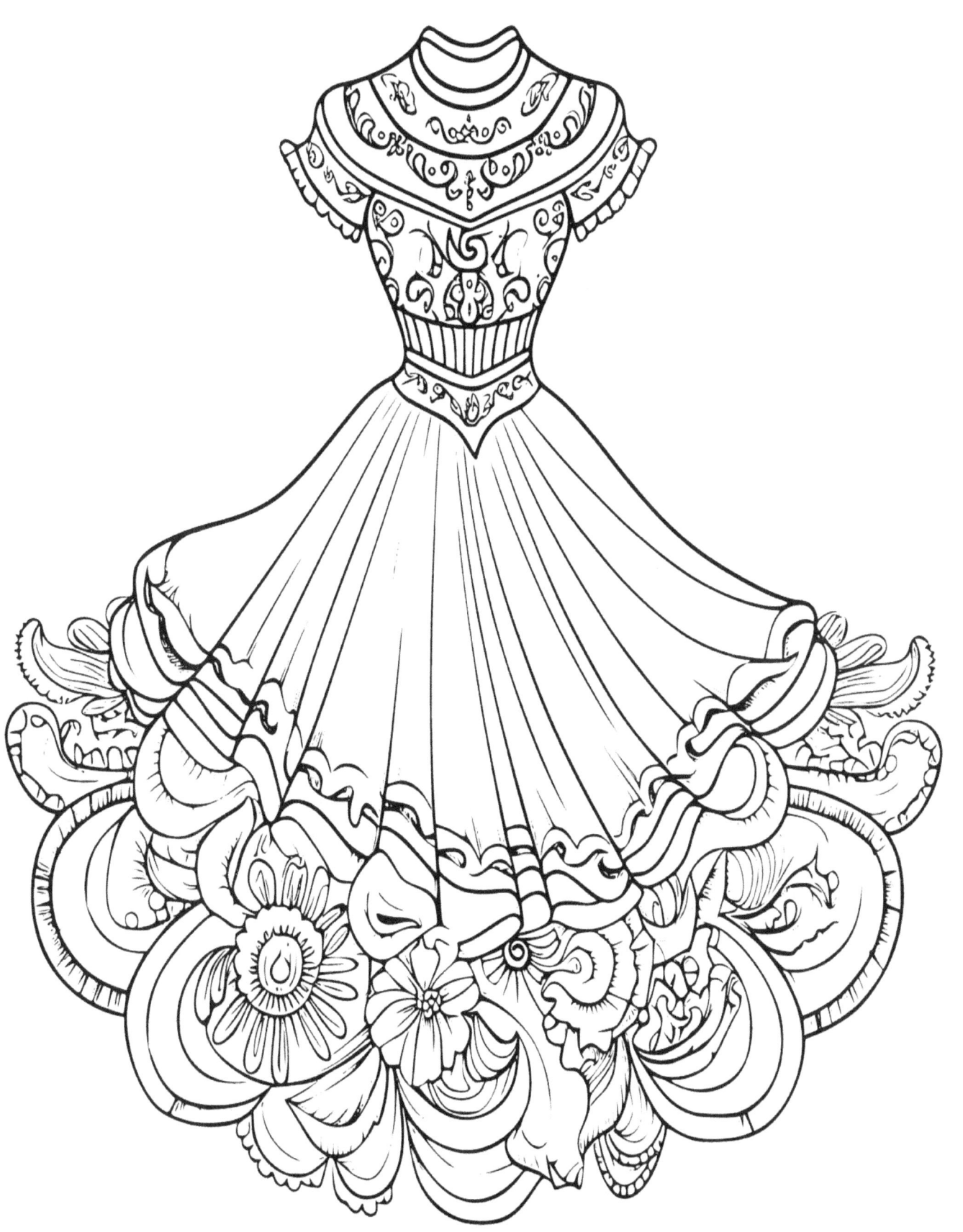

Intentionally Blank
Intencionalmente Blanco

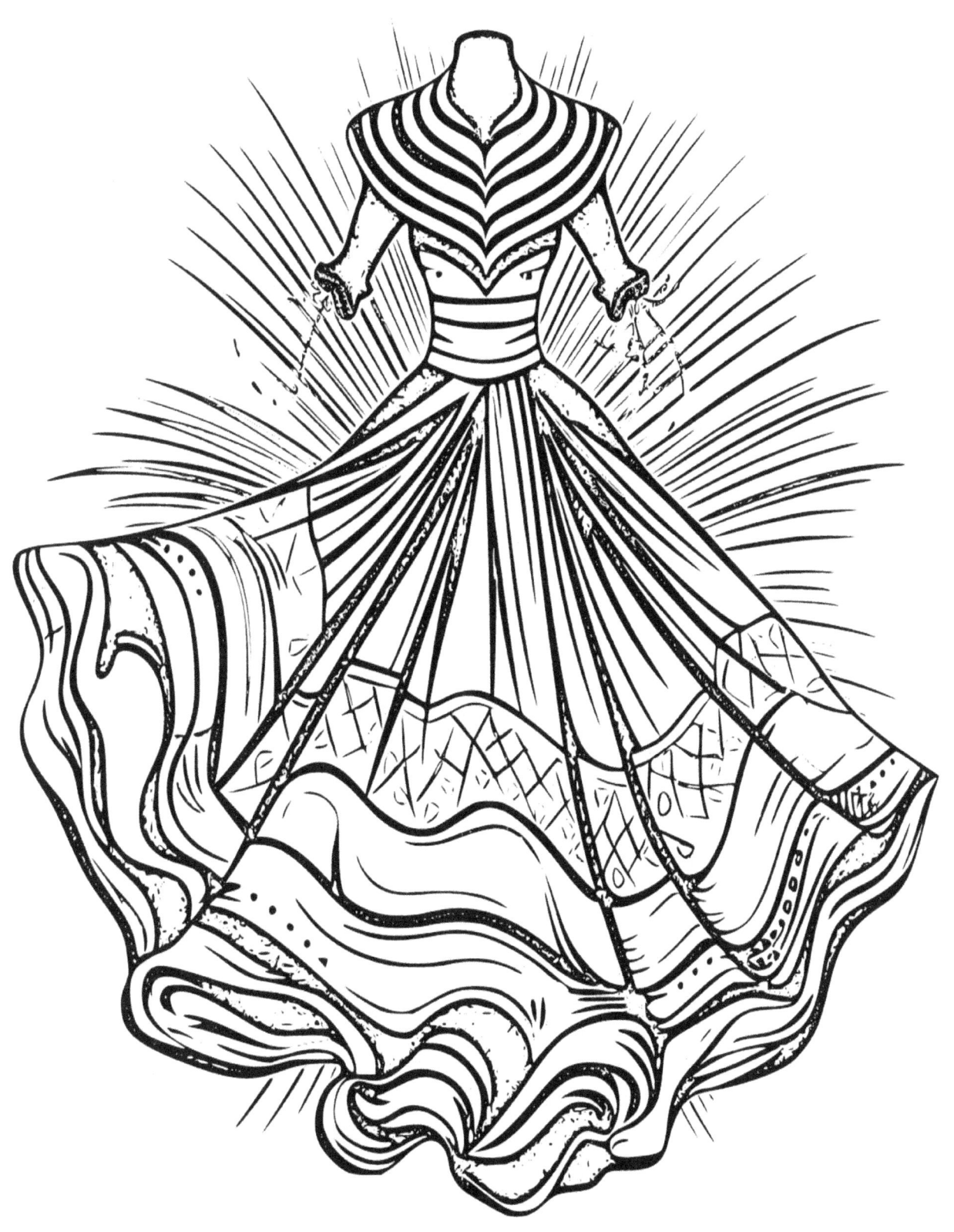

Intentionally Blank
Intencionalmente Blanco

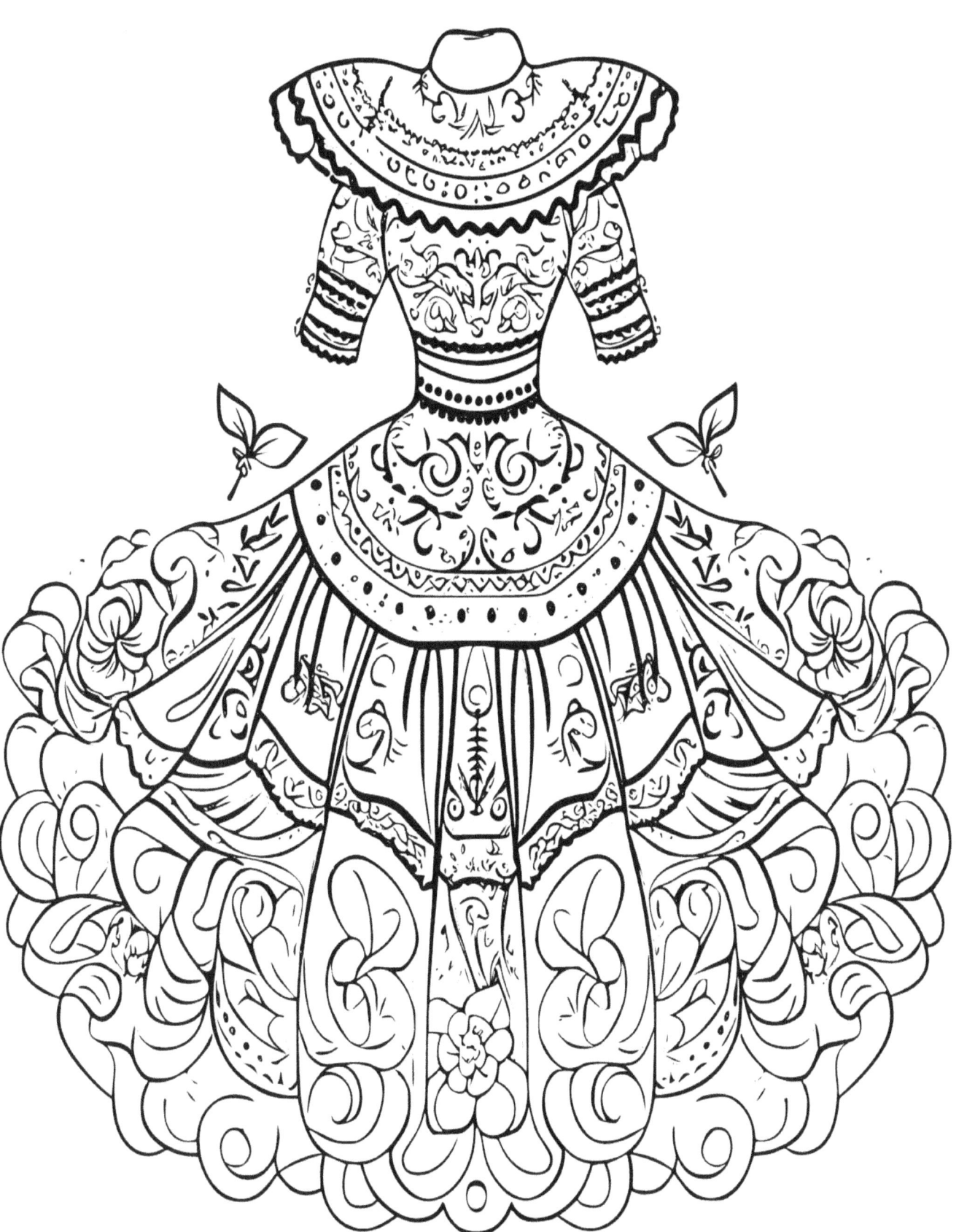

Intentionally Blank
Intencionalmente Blanco

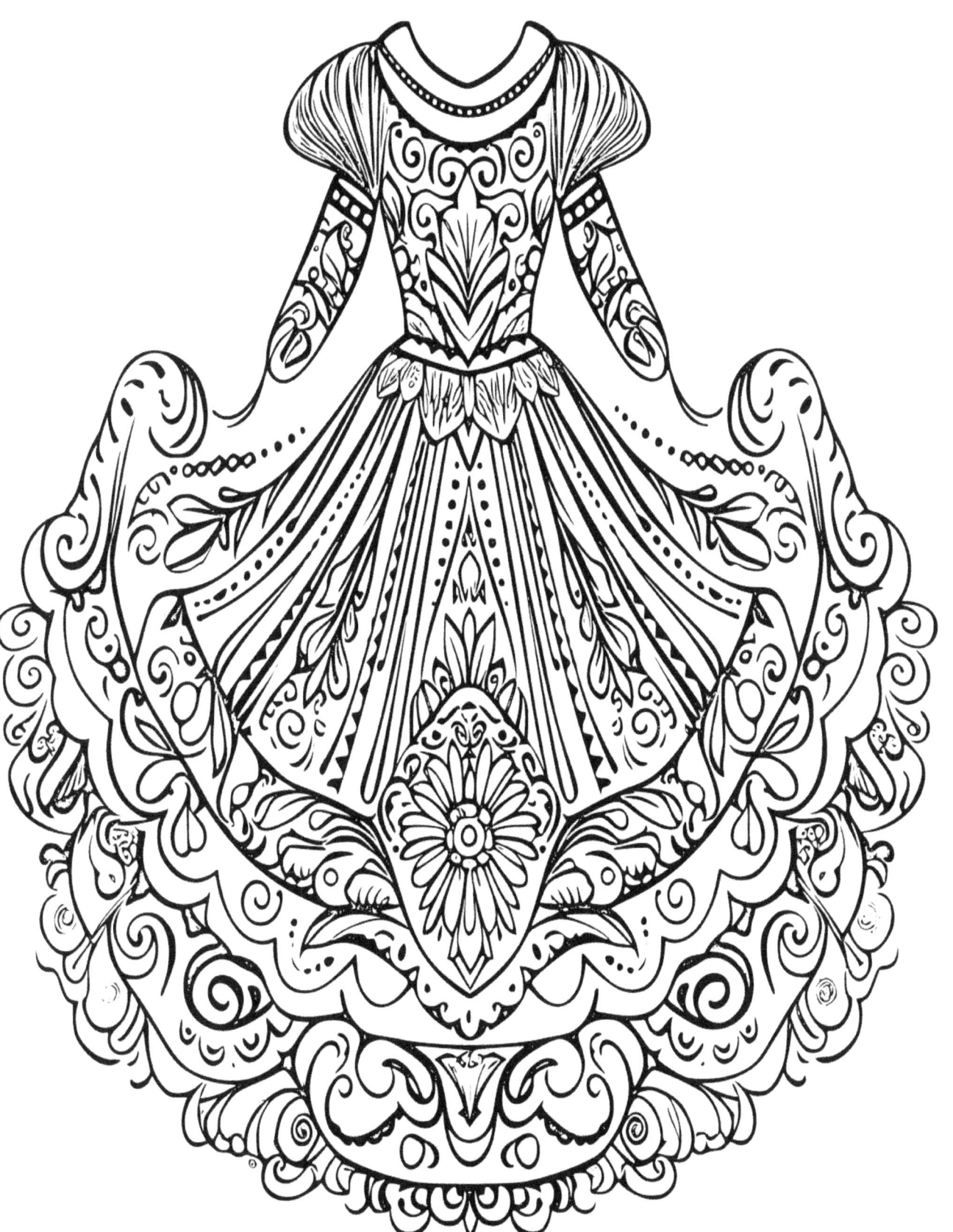

Intentionally Blank
Intencionalmente Blanco

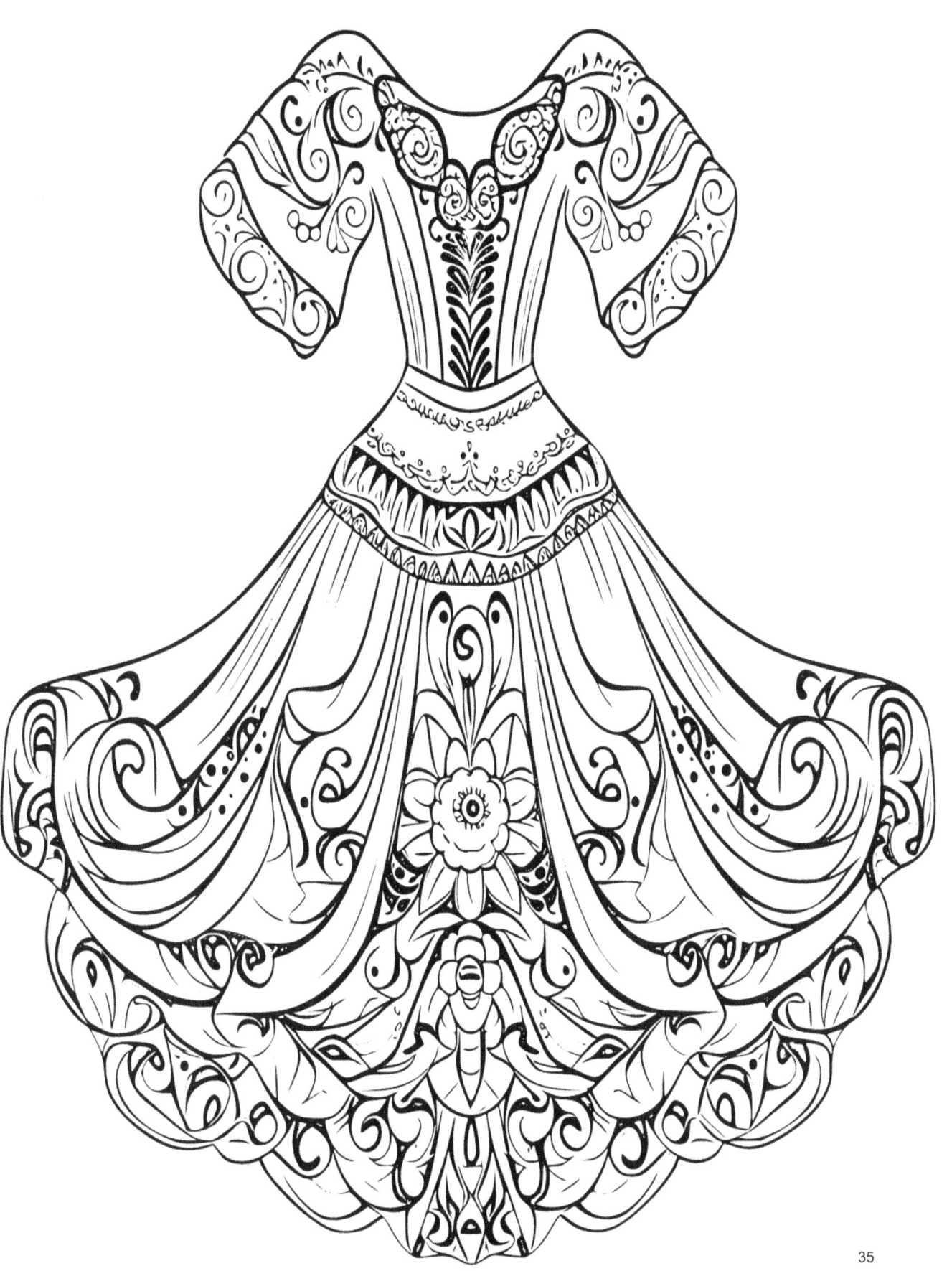

Intentionally Blank
Intencionalmente Blanco

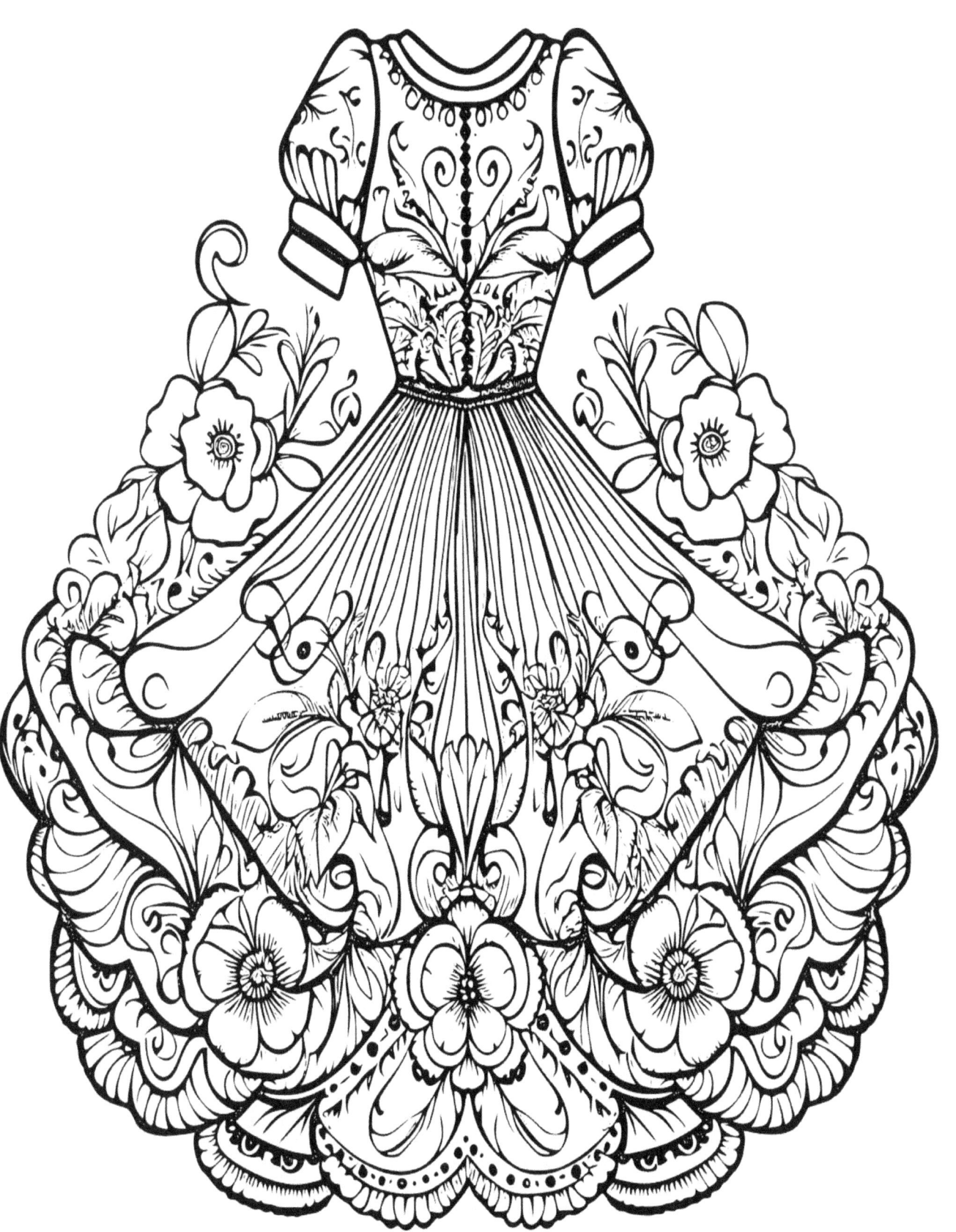

Intentionally Blank
Intencionalmente Blanco

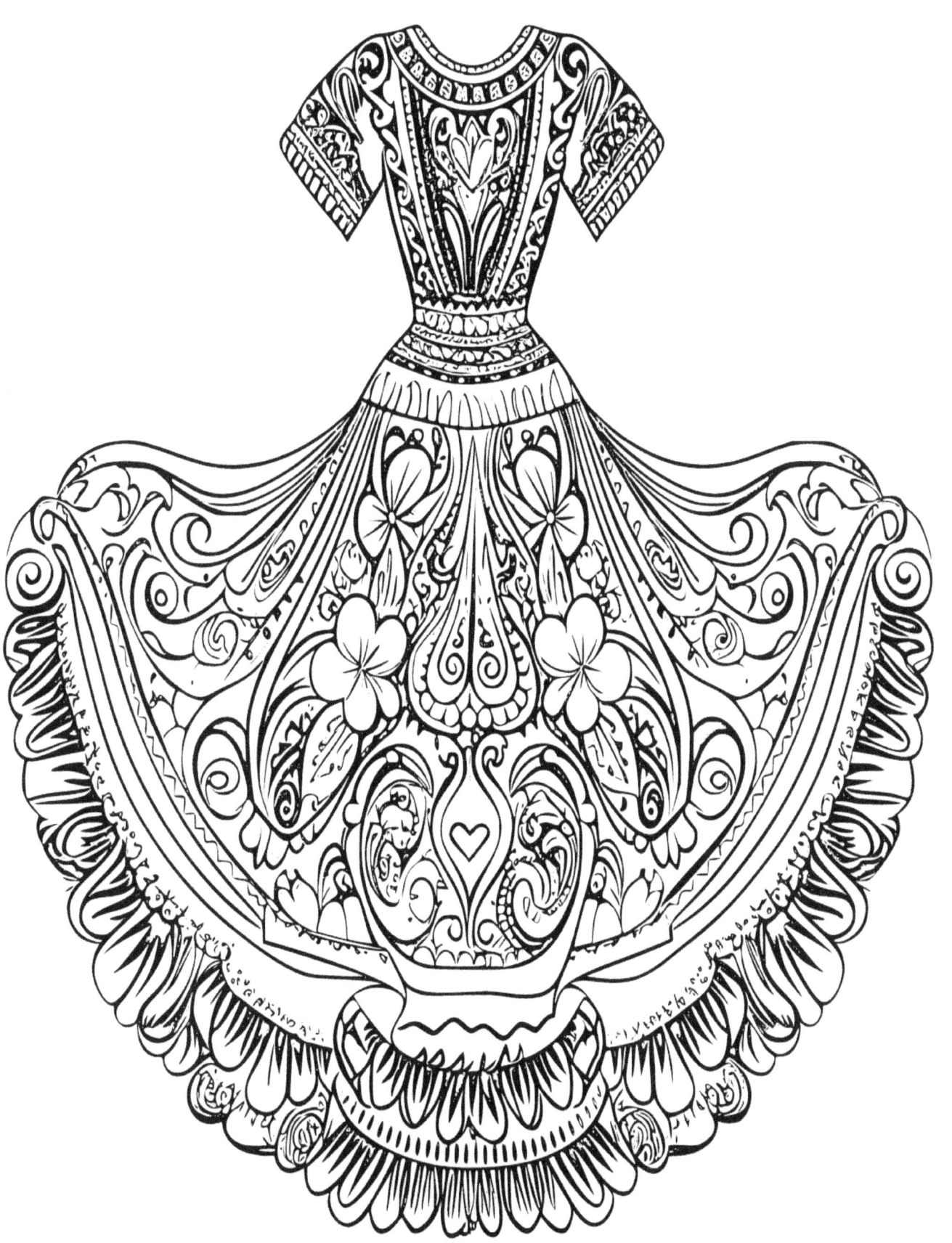

Intentionally Blank
Intencionalmente Blanco

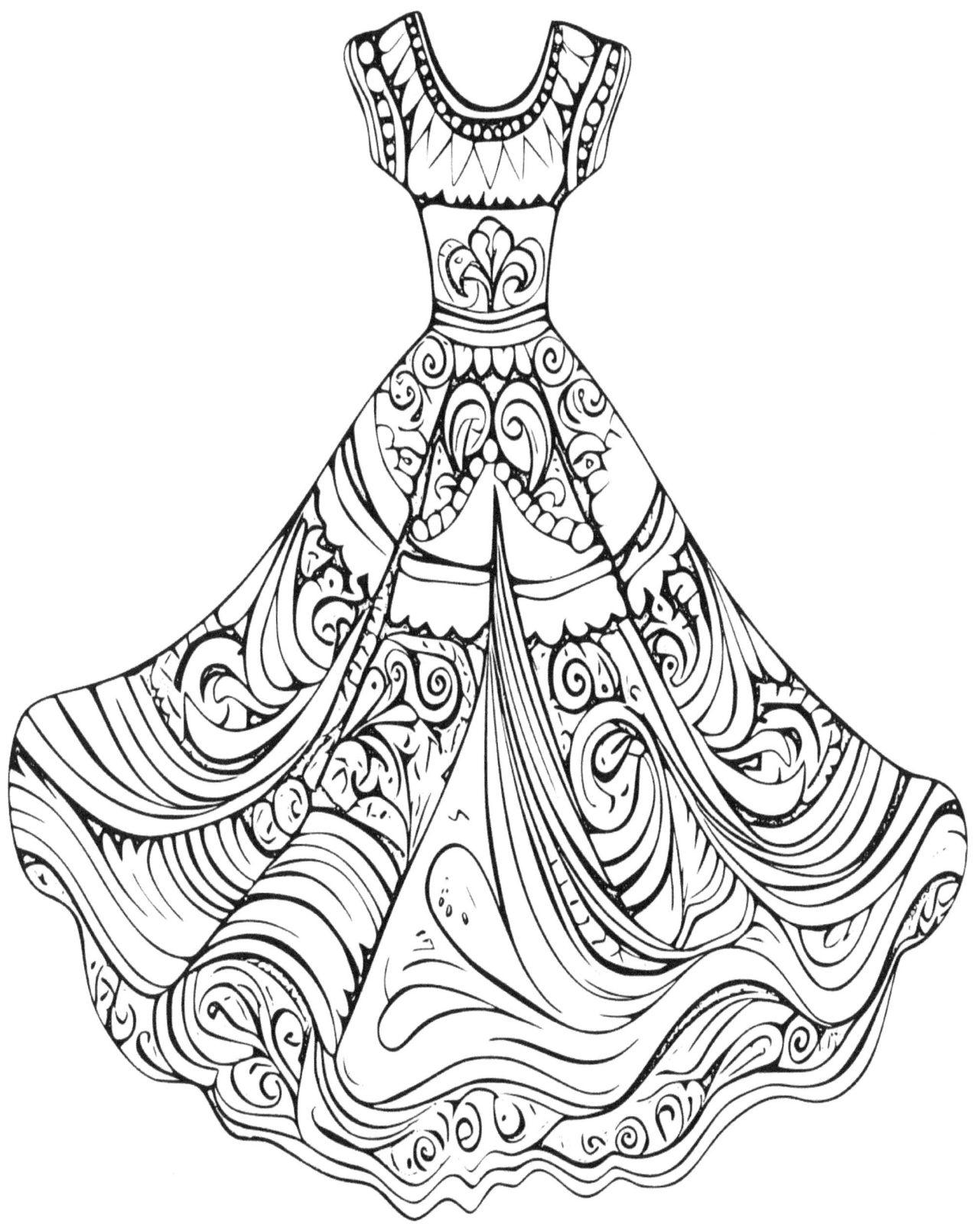

Intentionally Blank
Intencionalmente Blanco

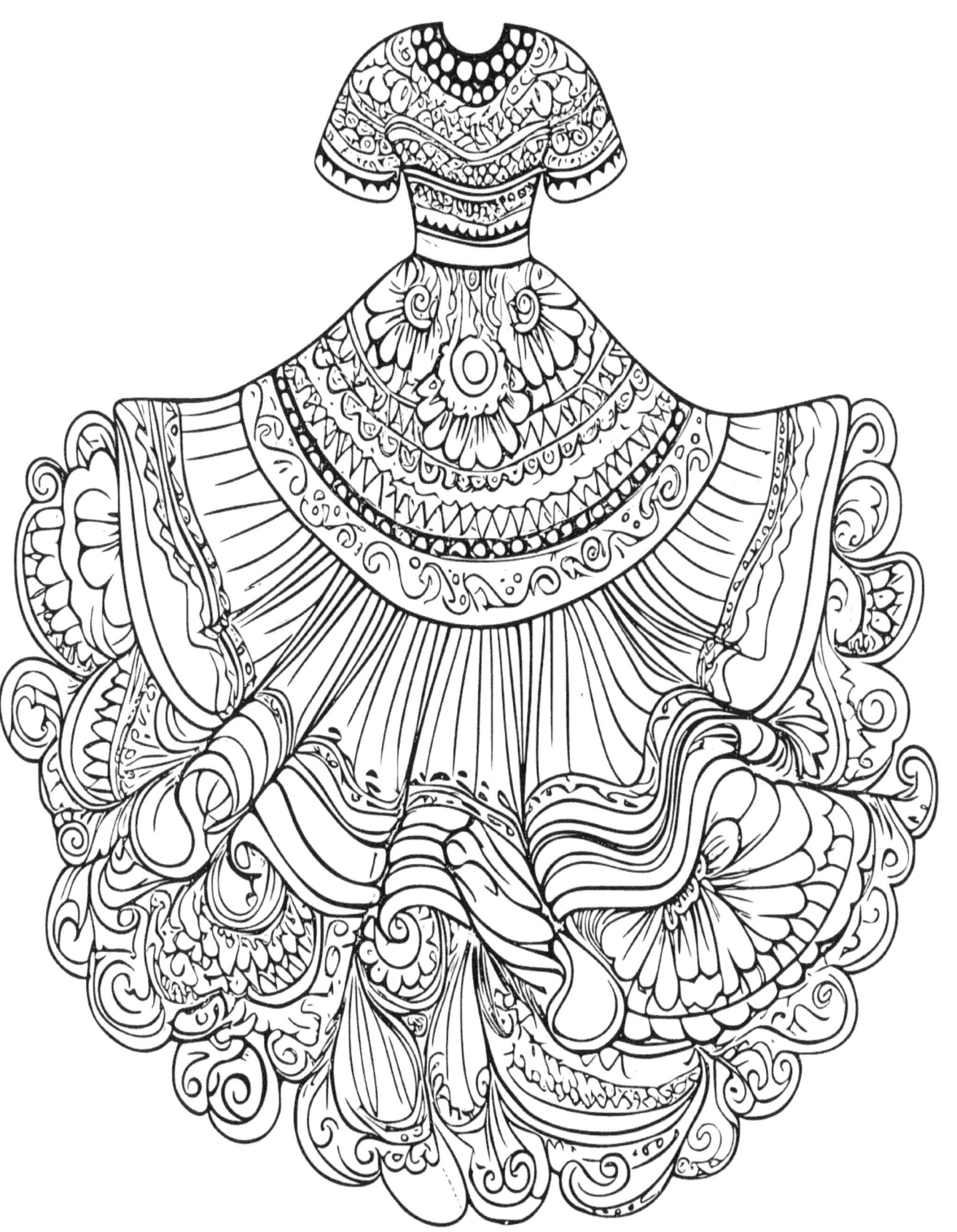

Intentionally Blank
Intencionalmente Blanco

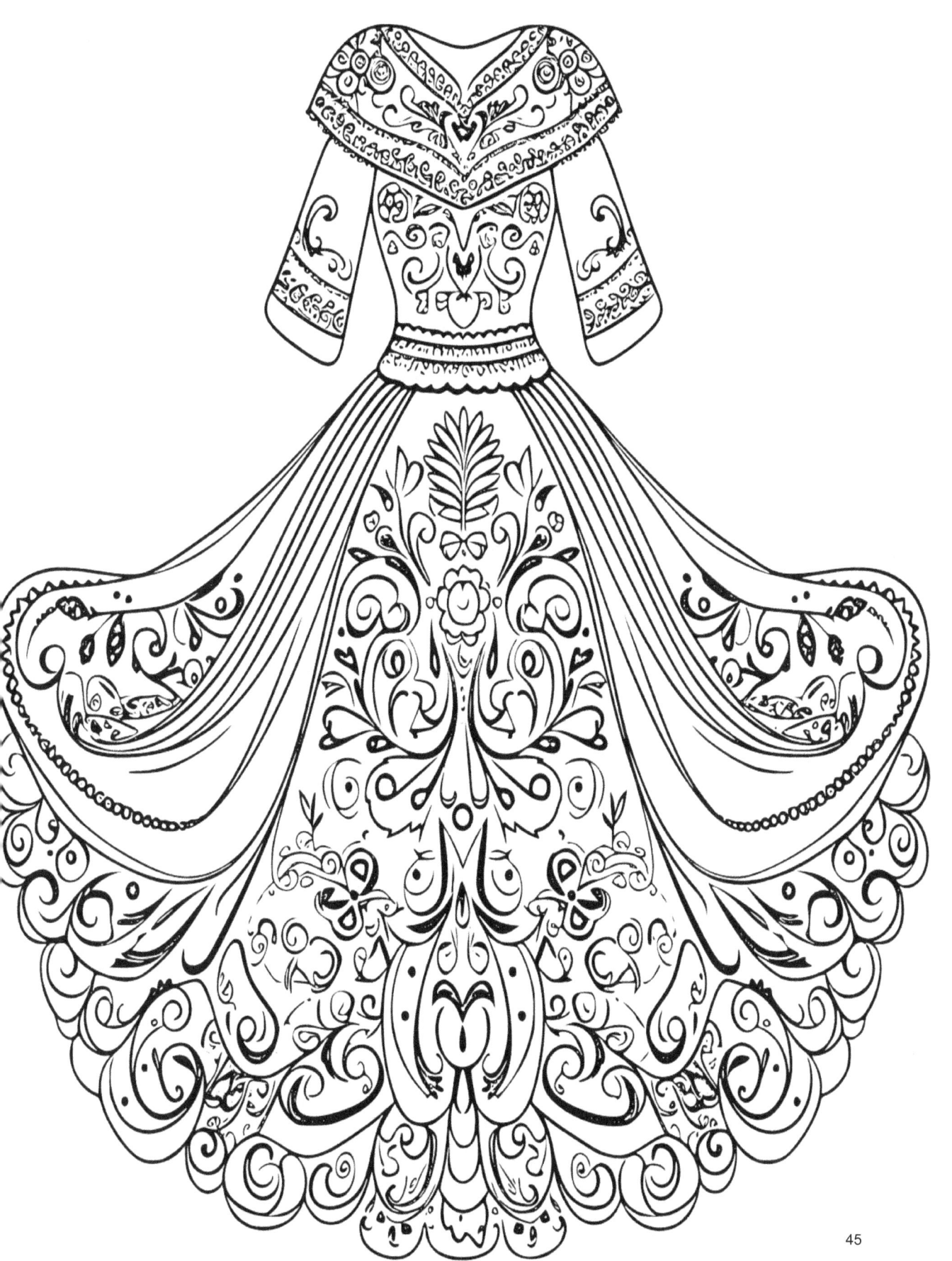

Intentionally Blank
Intencionalmente Blanco

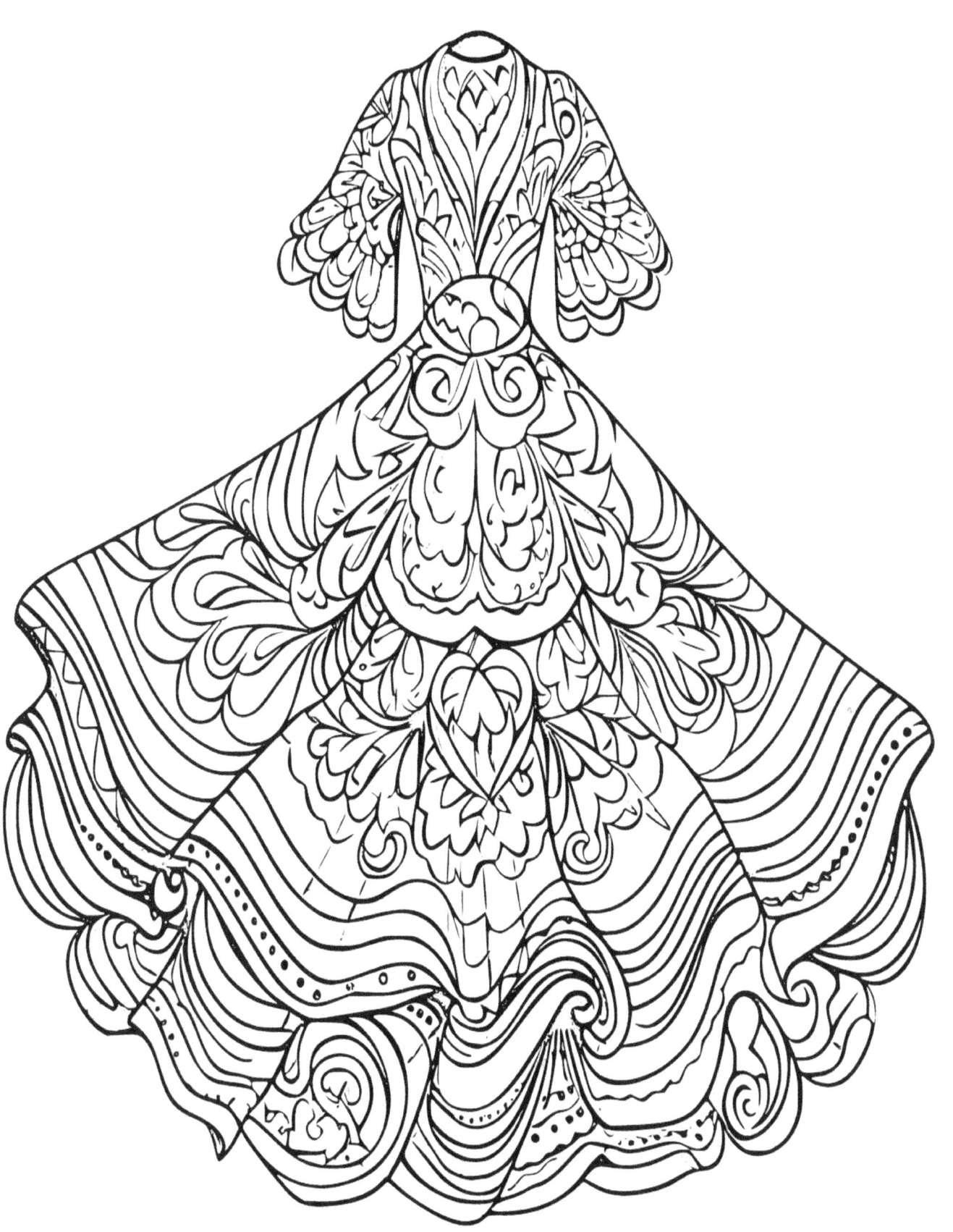

Intentionally Blank
Intencionalmente Blanco

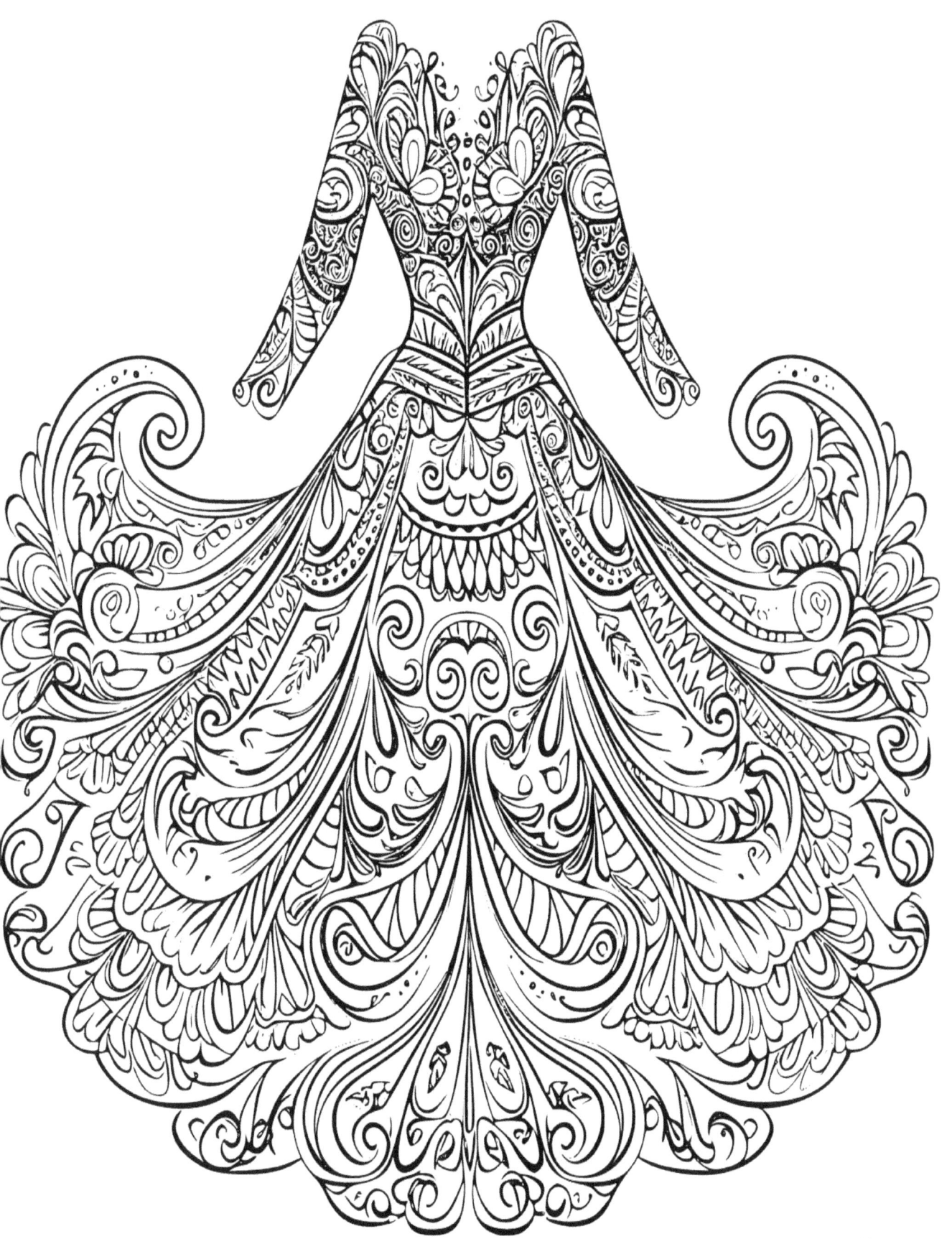

Intentionally Blank
Intencionalmente Blanco

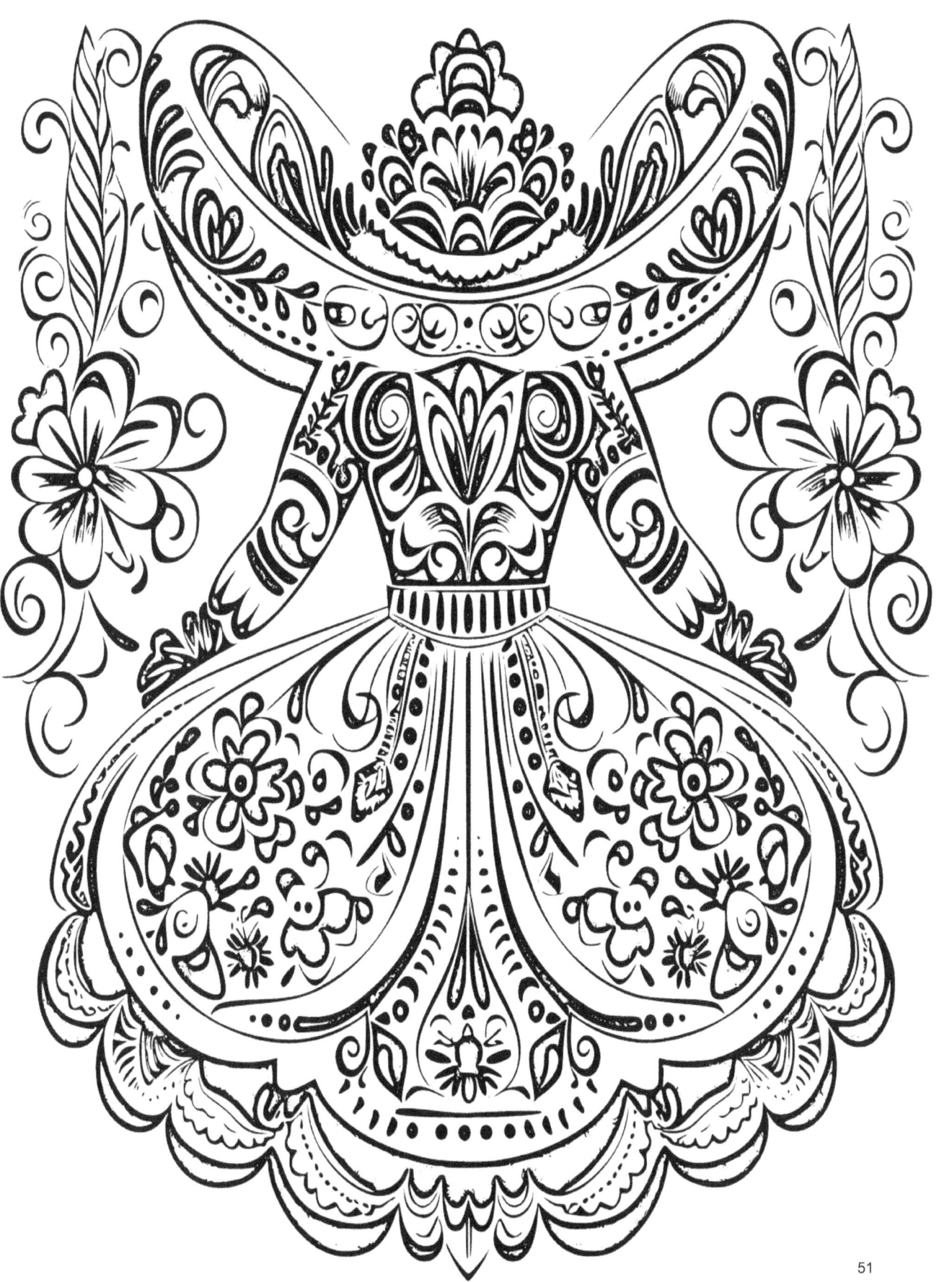

Intentionally Blank
Intencionalmente Blanco

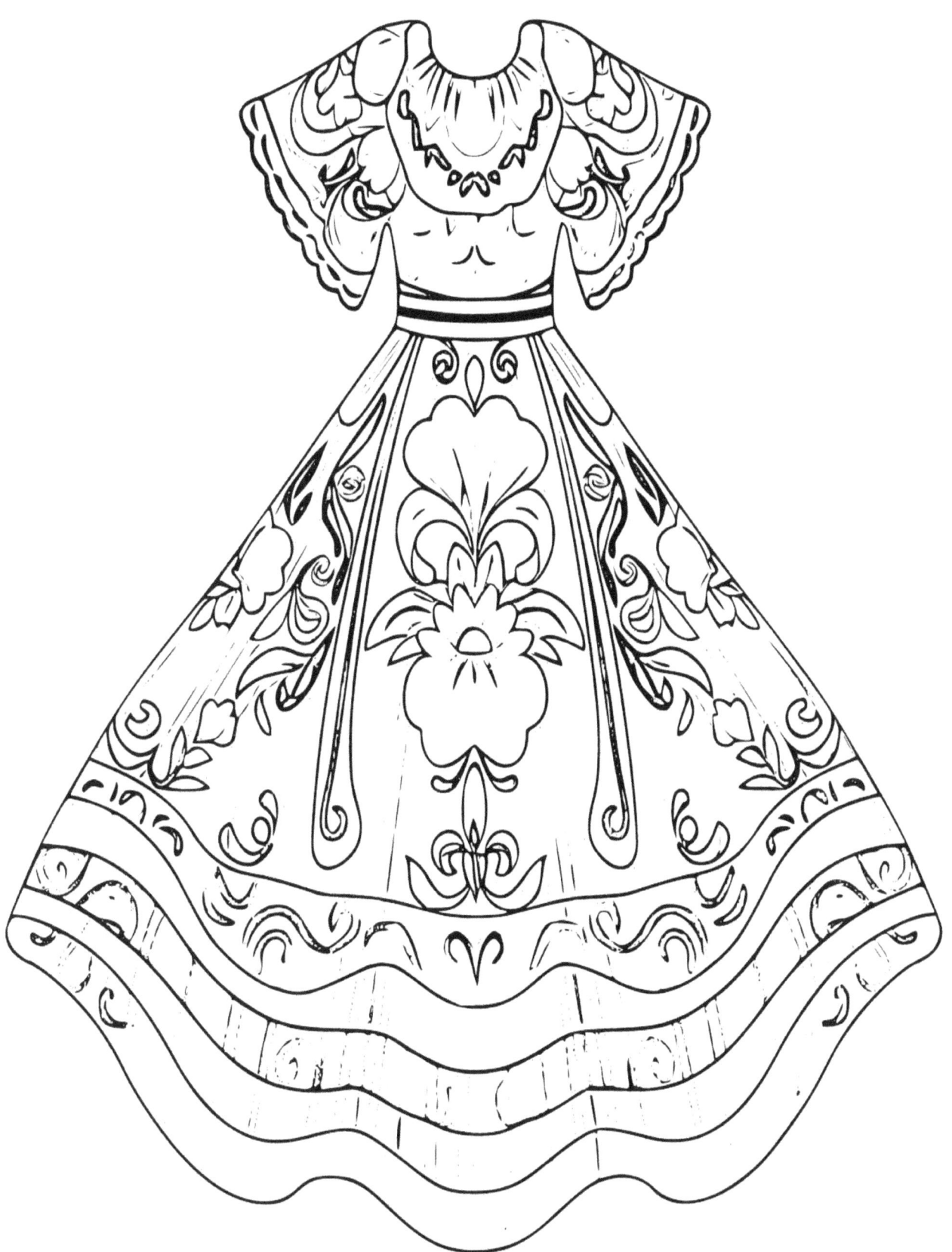

Intentionally Blank
Intencionalmente Blanco

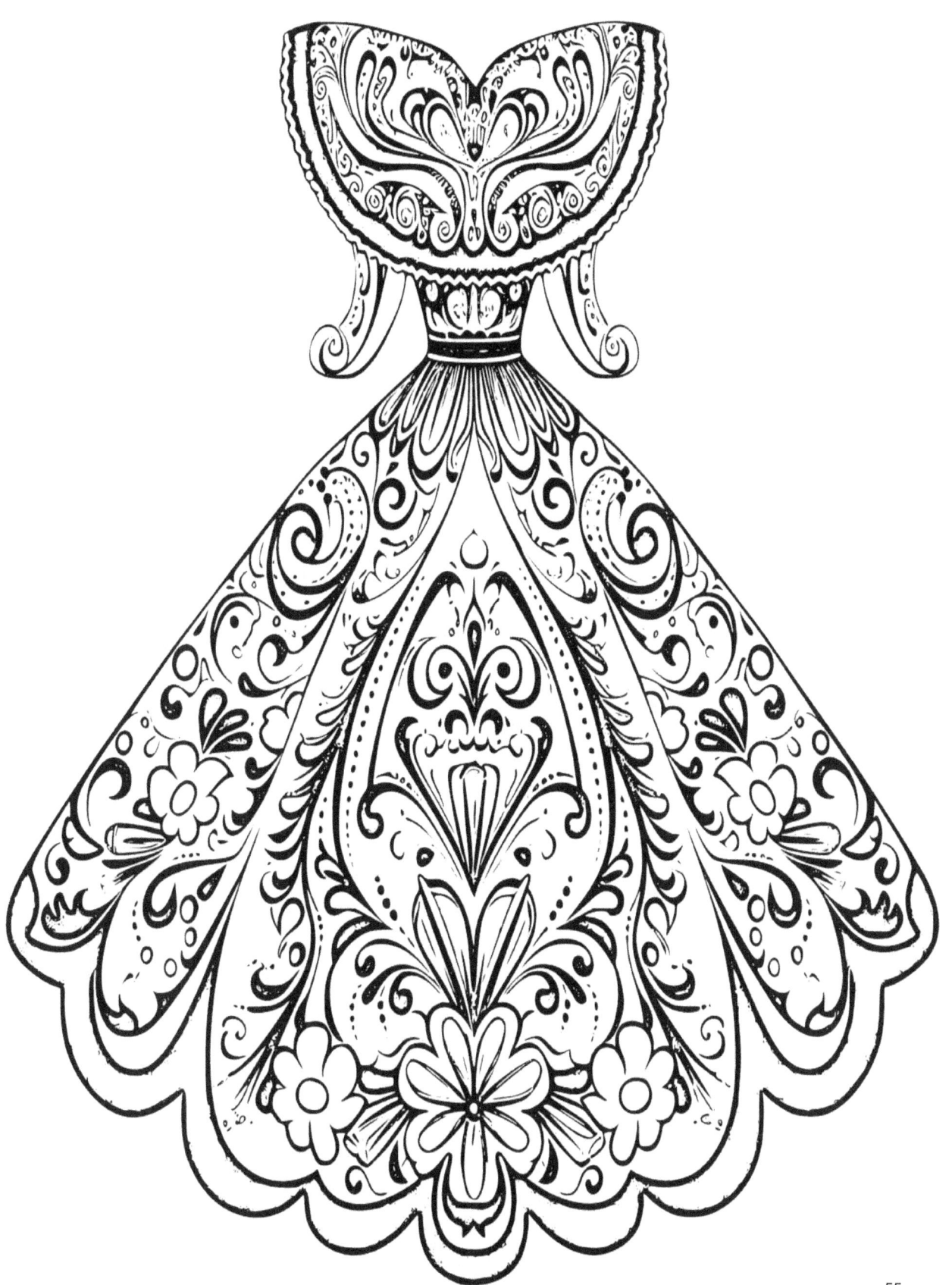

Intentionally Blank
Intencionalmente Blanco

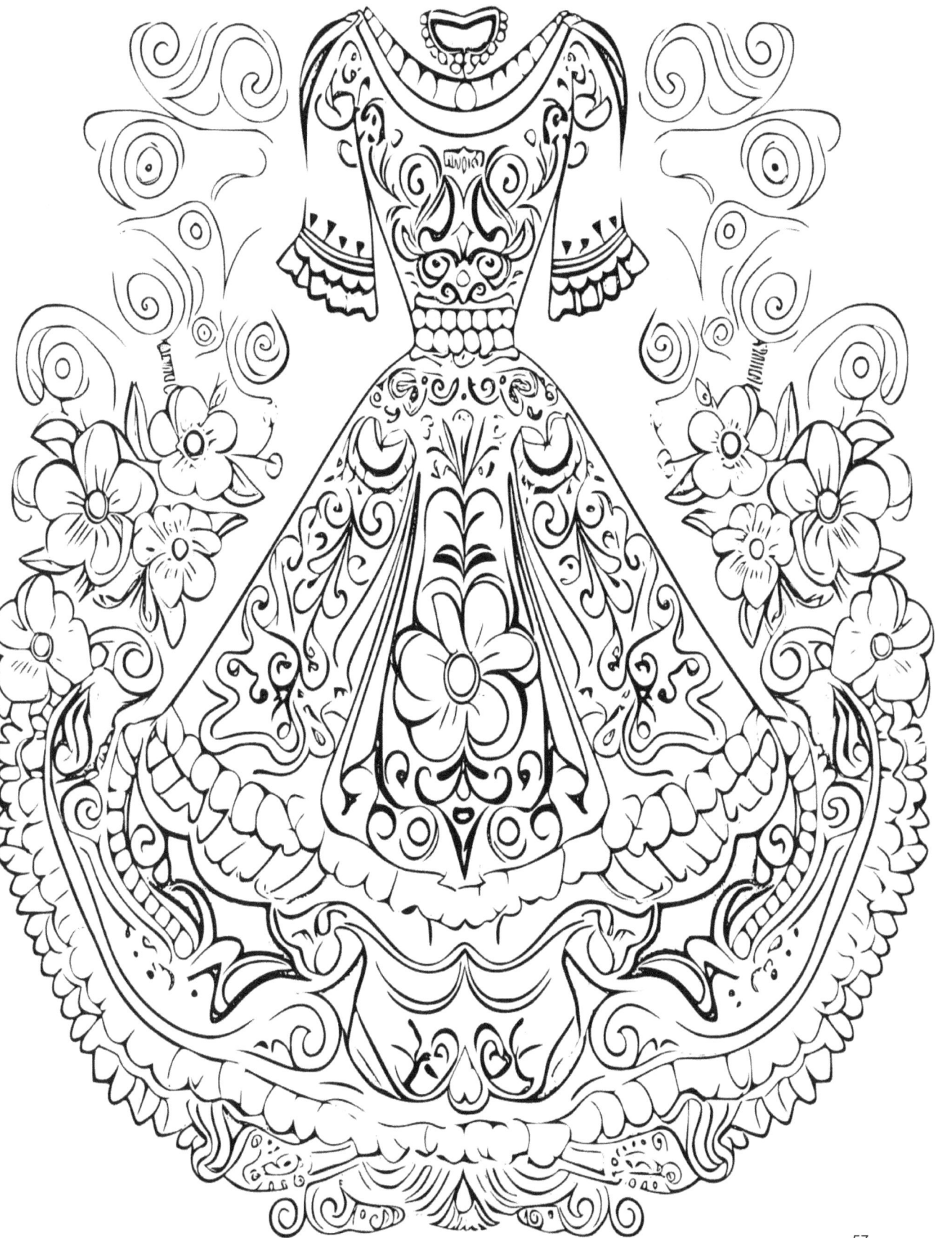

Intentionally Blank
Intencionalmente Blanco

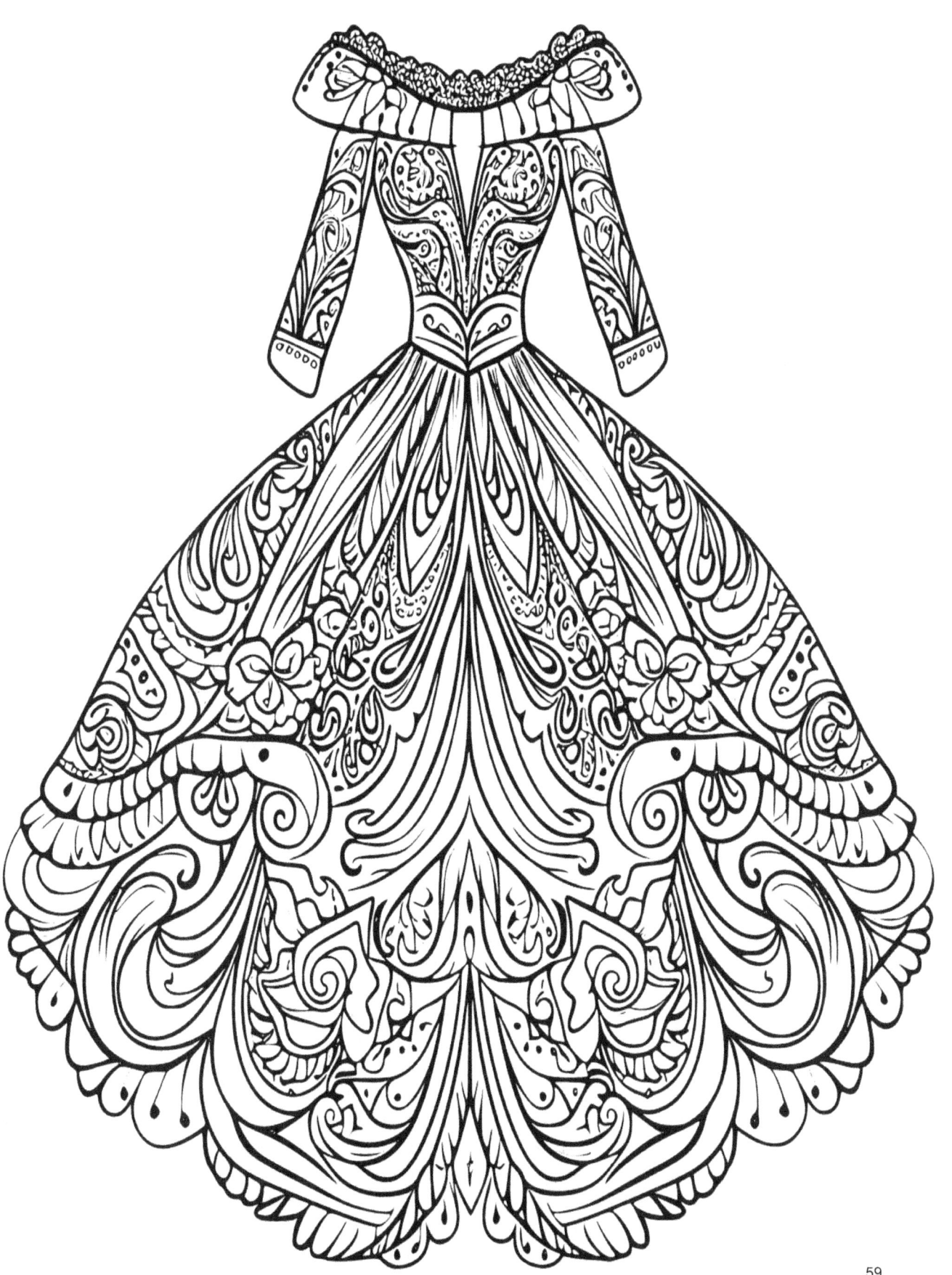

Intentionally Blank
Intencionalmente Blanco

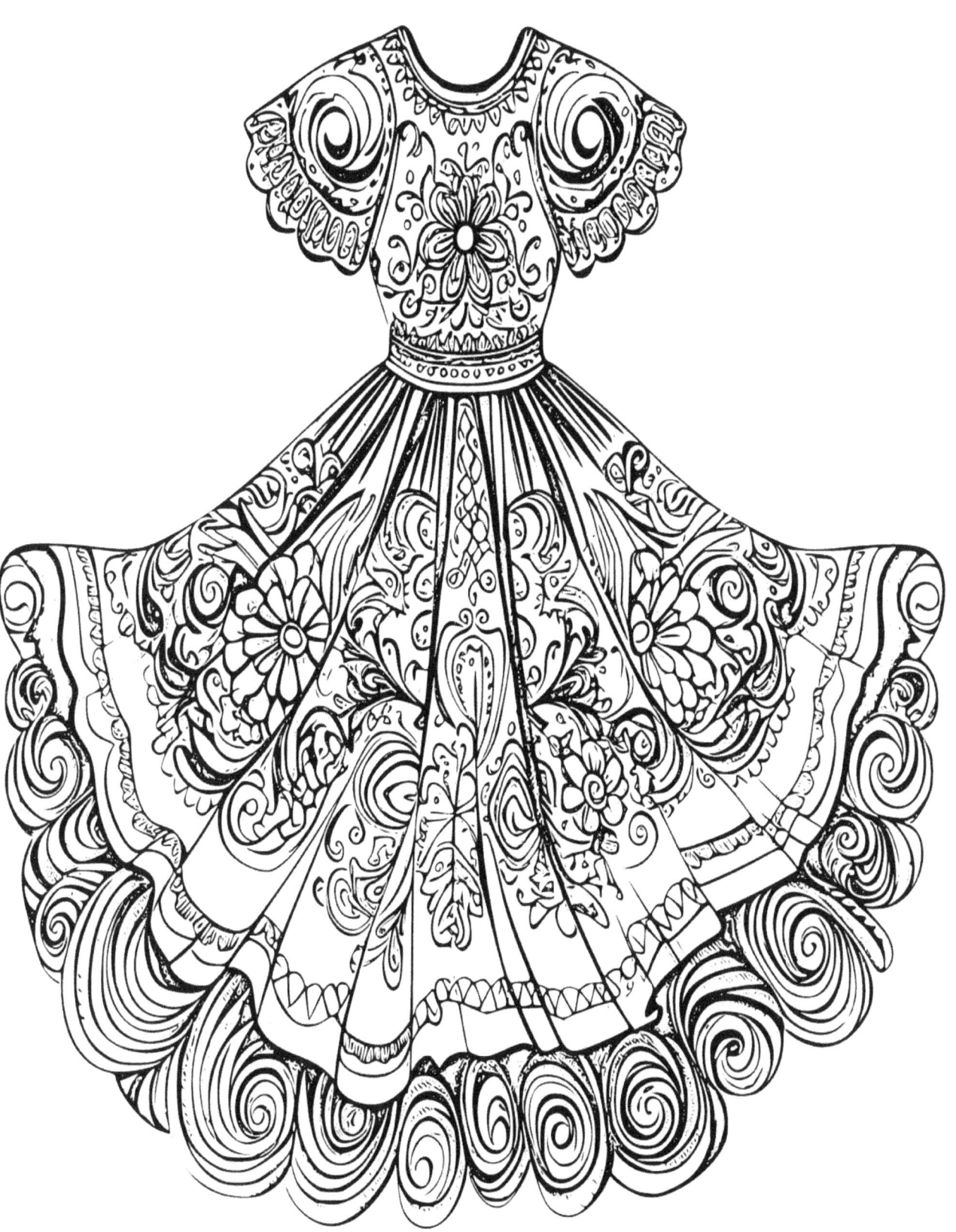

Intentionally Blank
Intencionalmente Blanco

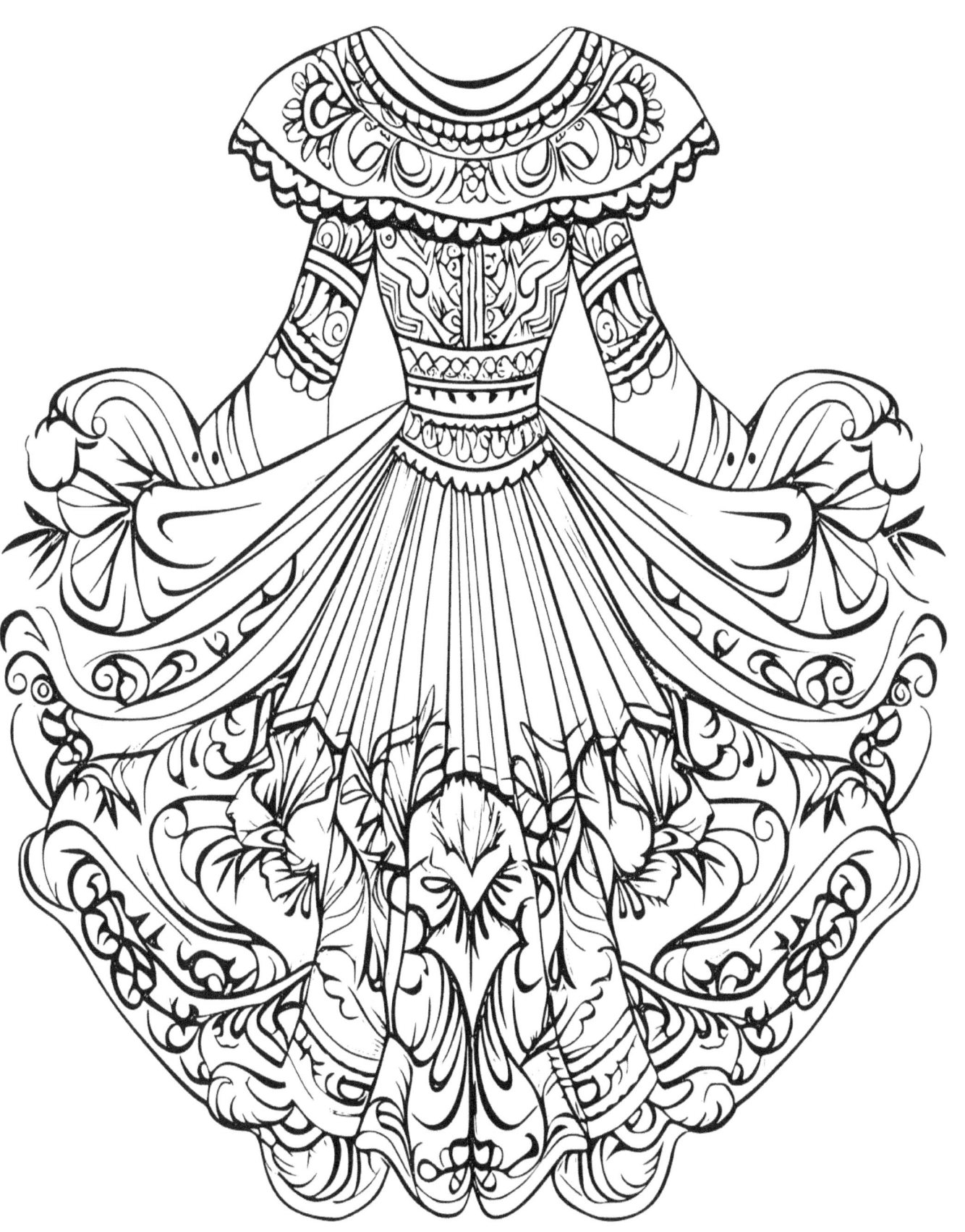

Intentionally Blank
Intencionalmente Blanco

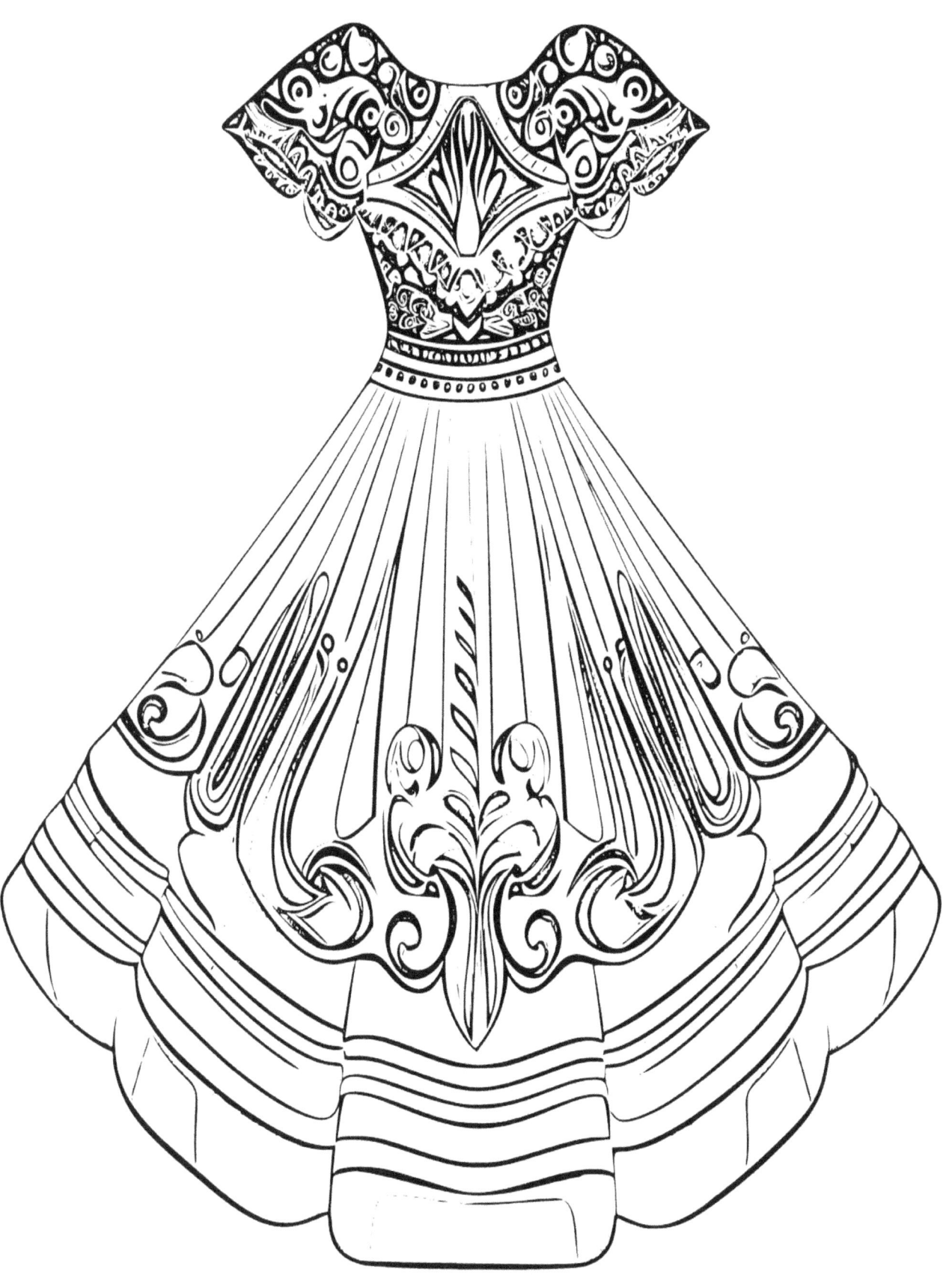

Intentionally Blank
Intencionalmente Blanco

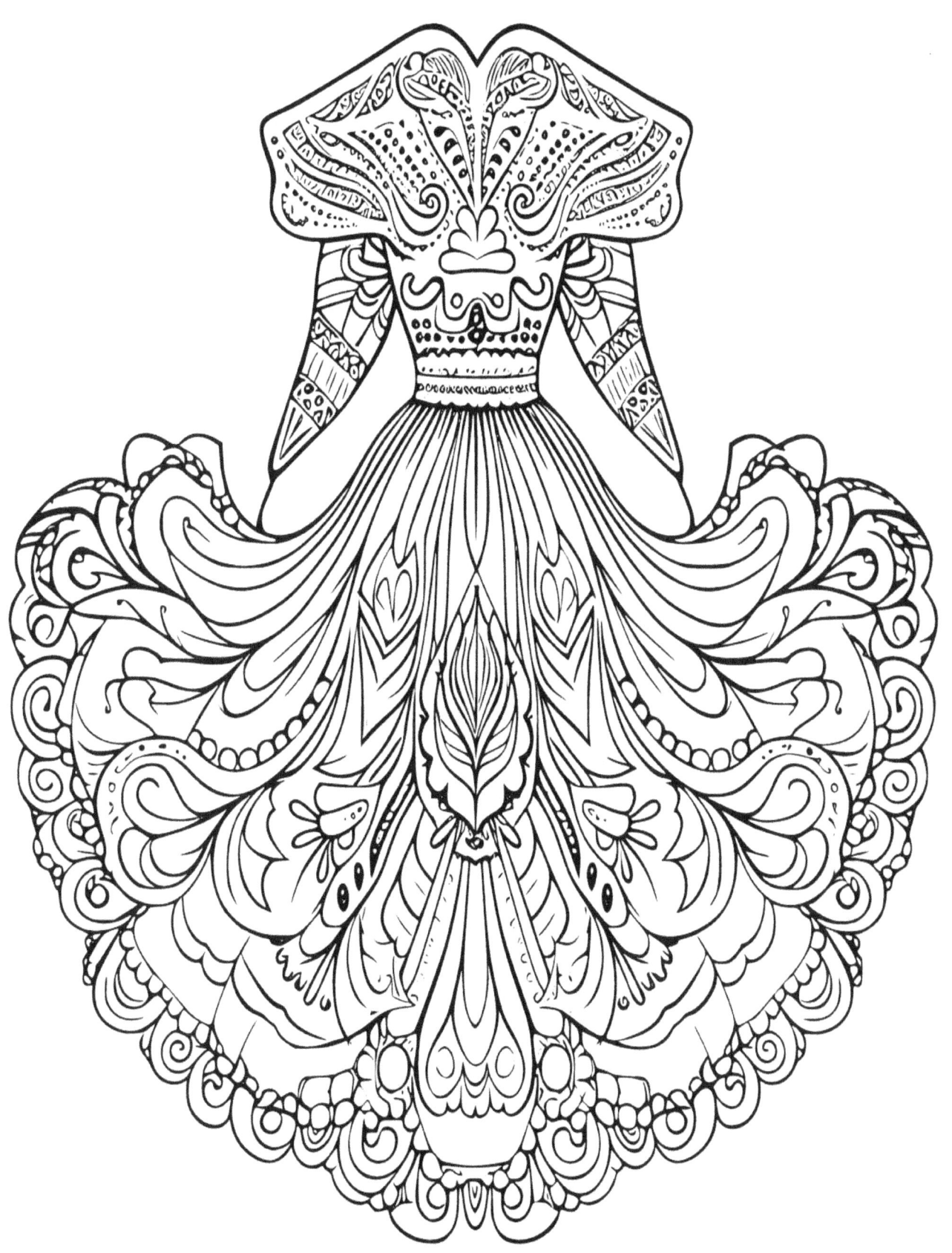

Intentionally Blank
Intencionalmente Blanco

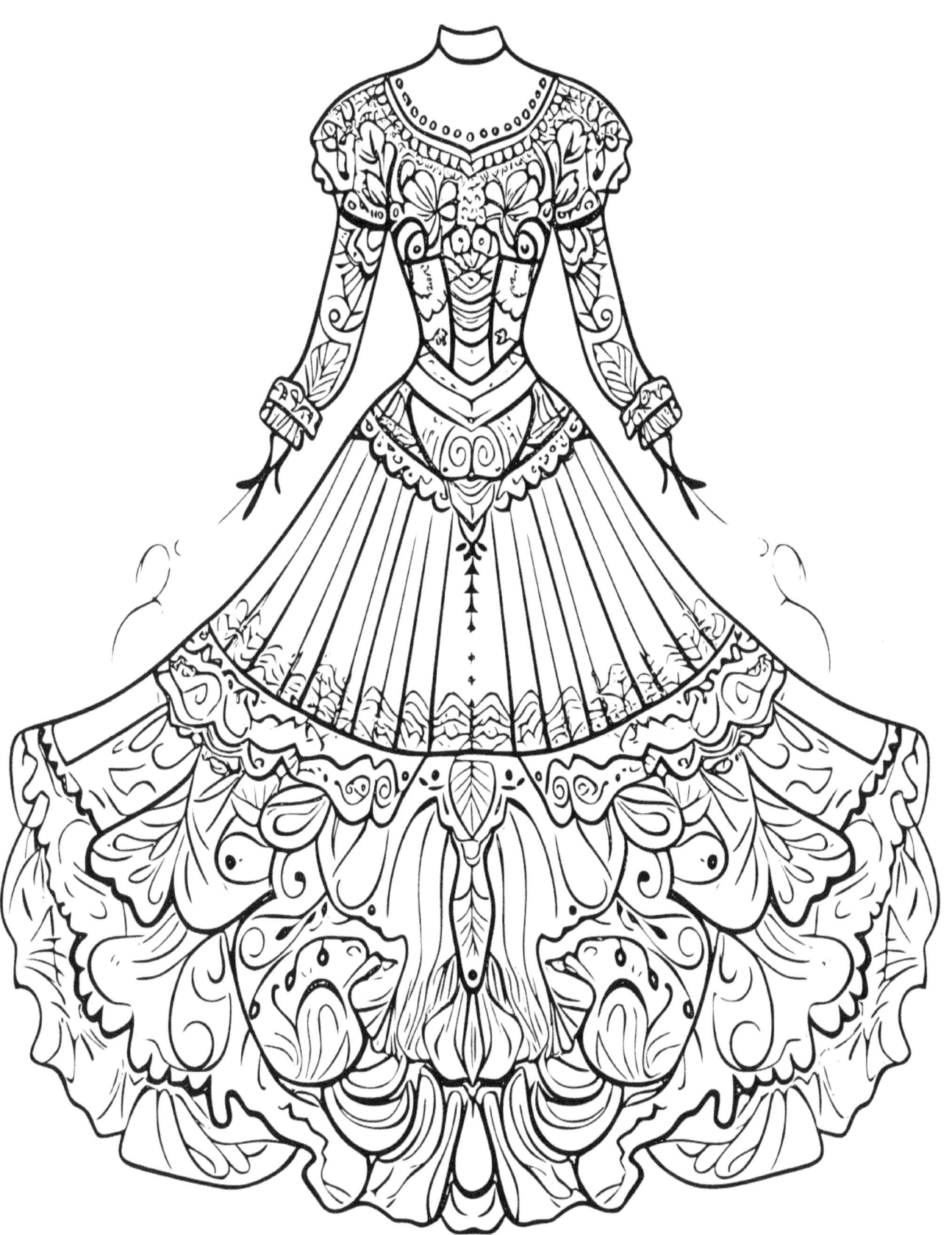

Intentionally Blank
Intencionalmente Blanco

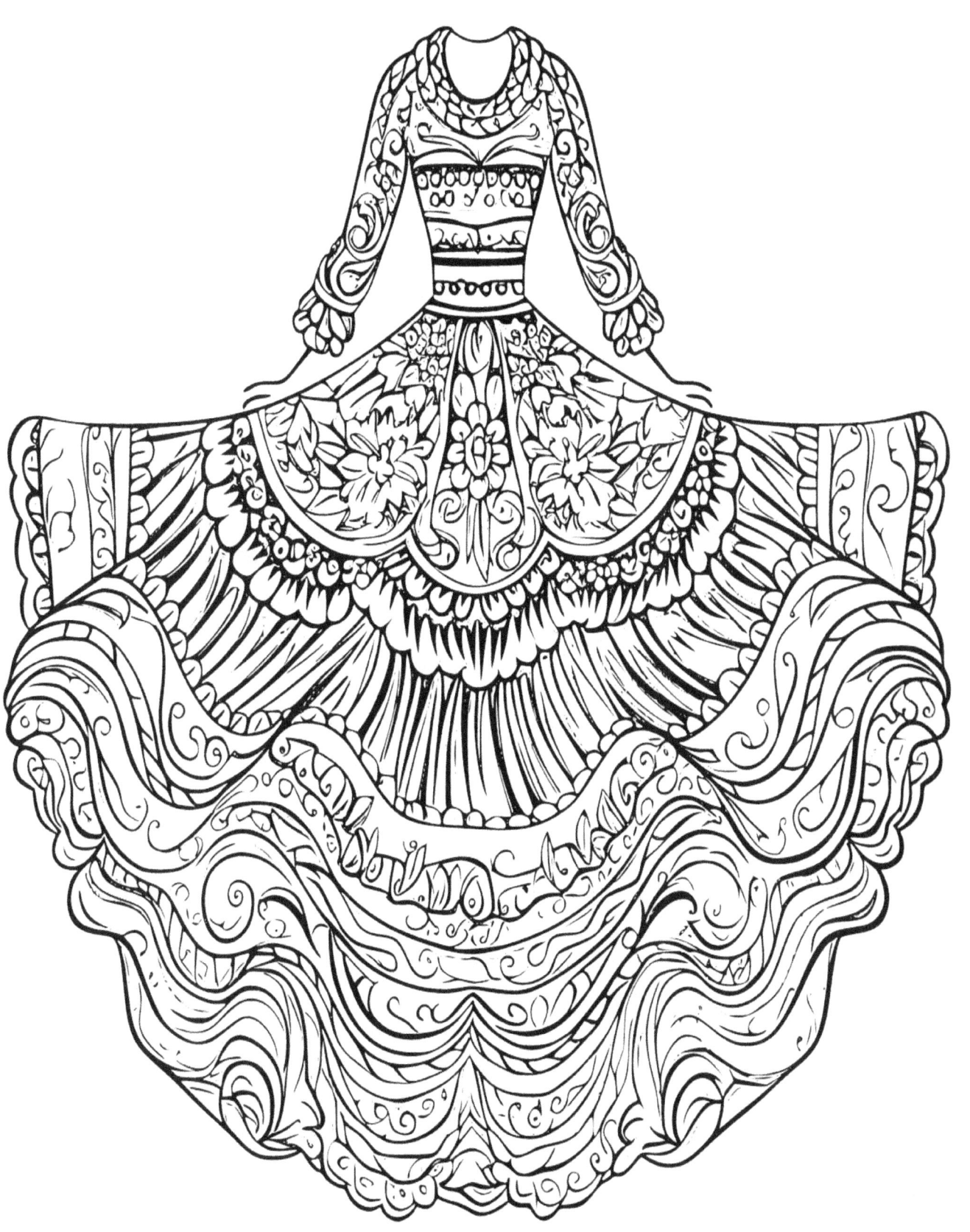

Intentionally Blank
Intencionalmente Blanco

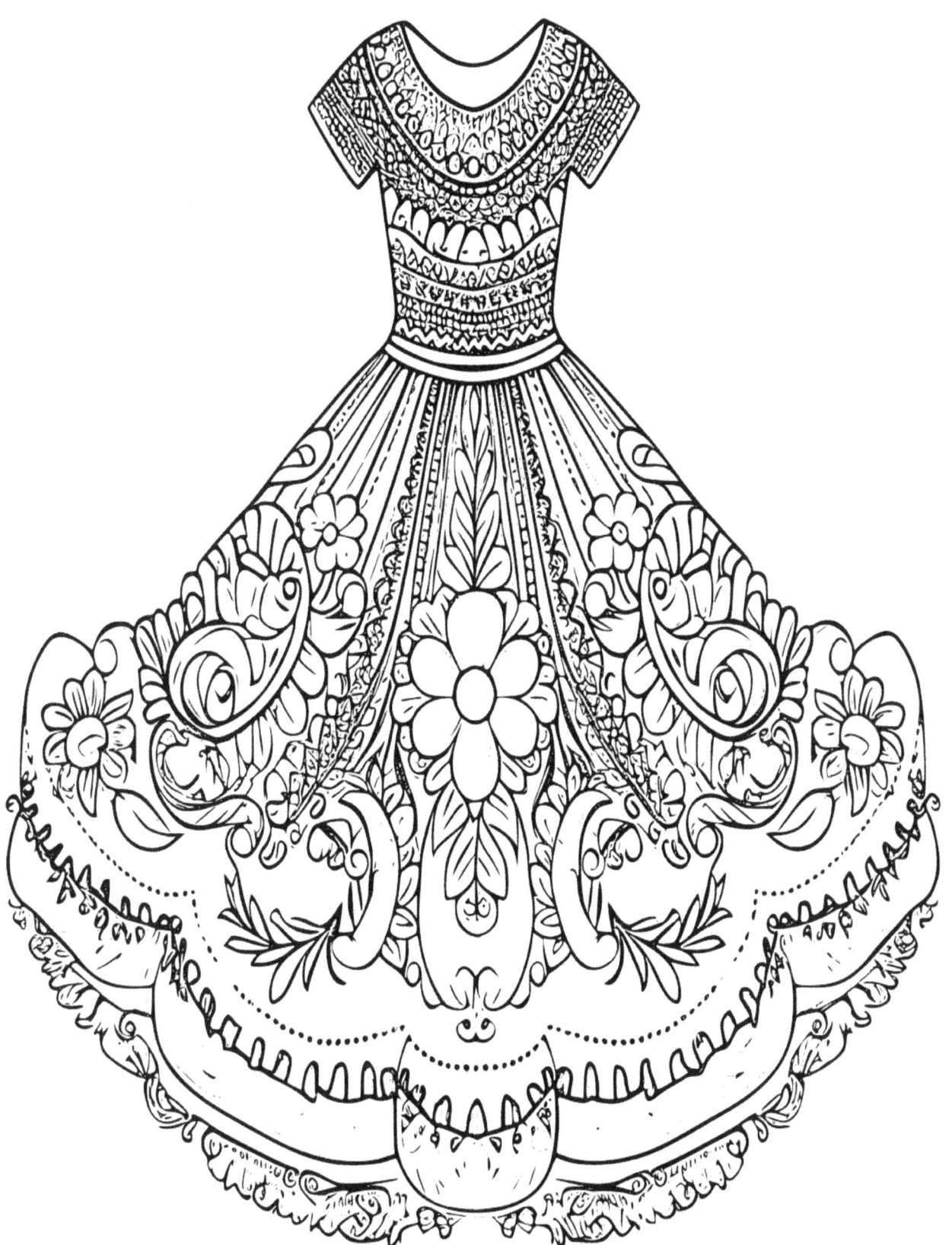

Intentionally Blank
Intencionalmente Blanco

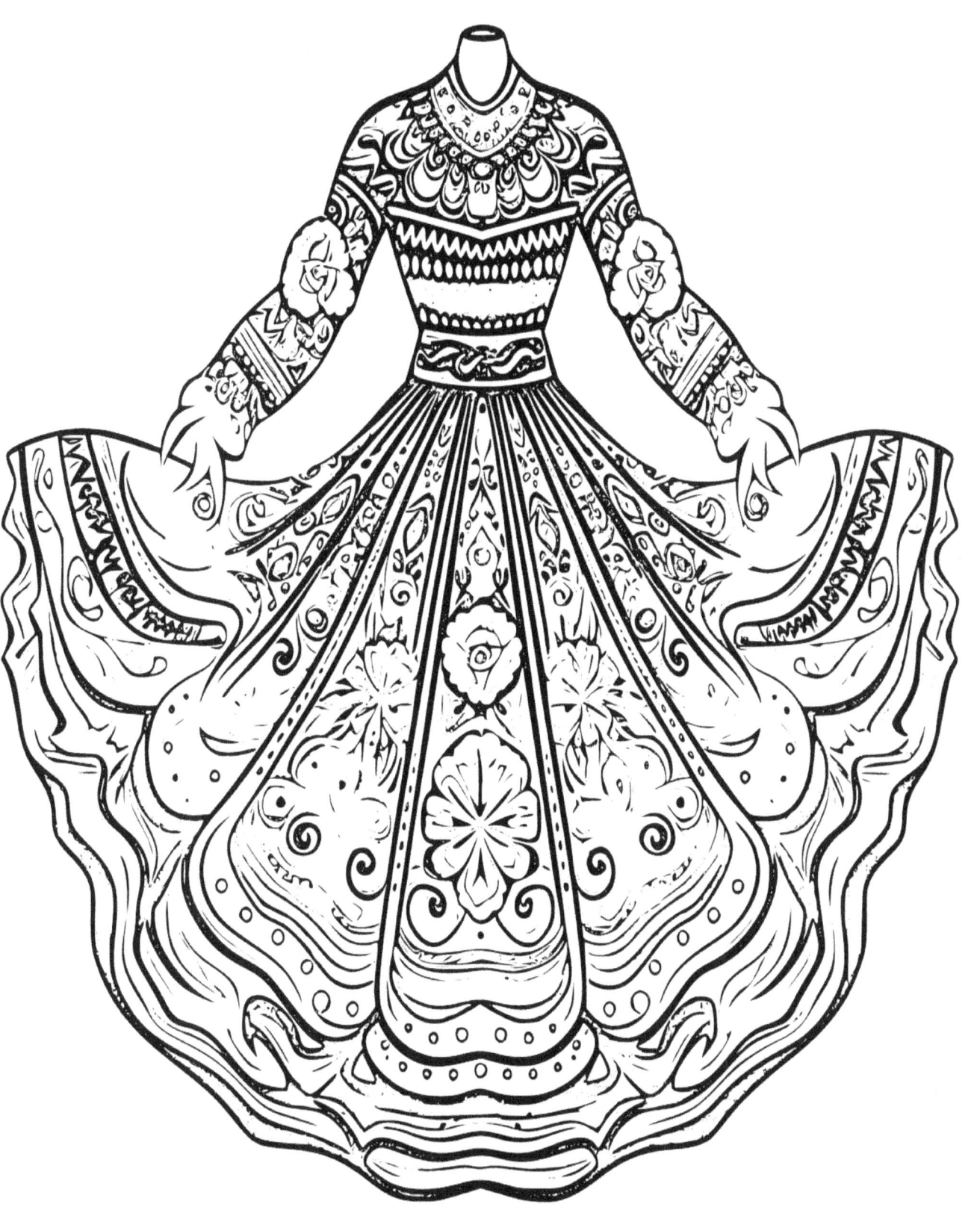

Intentionally Blank
Intencionalmente Blanco

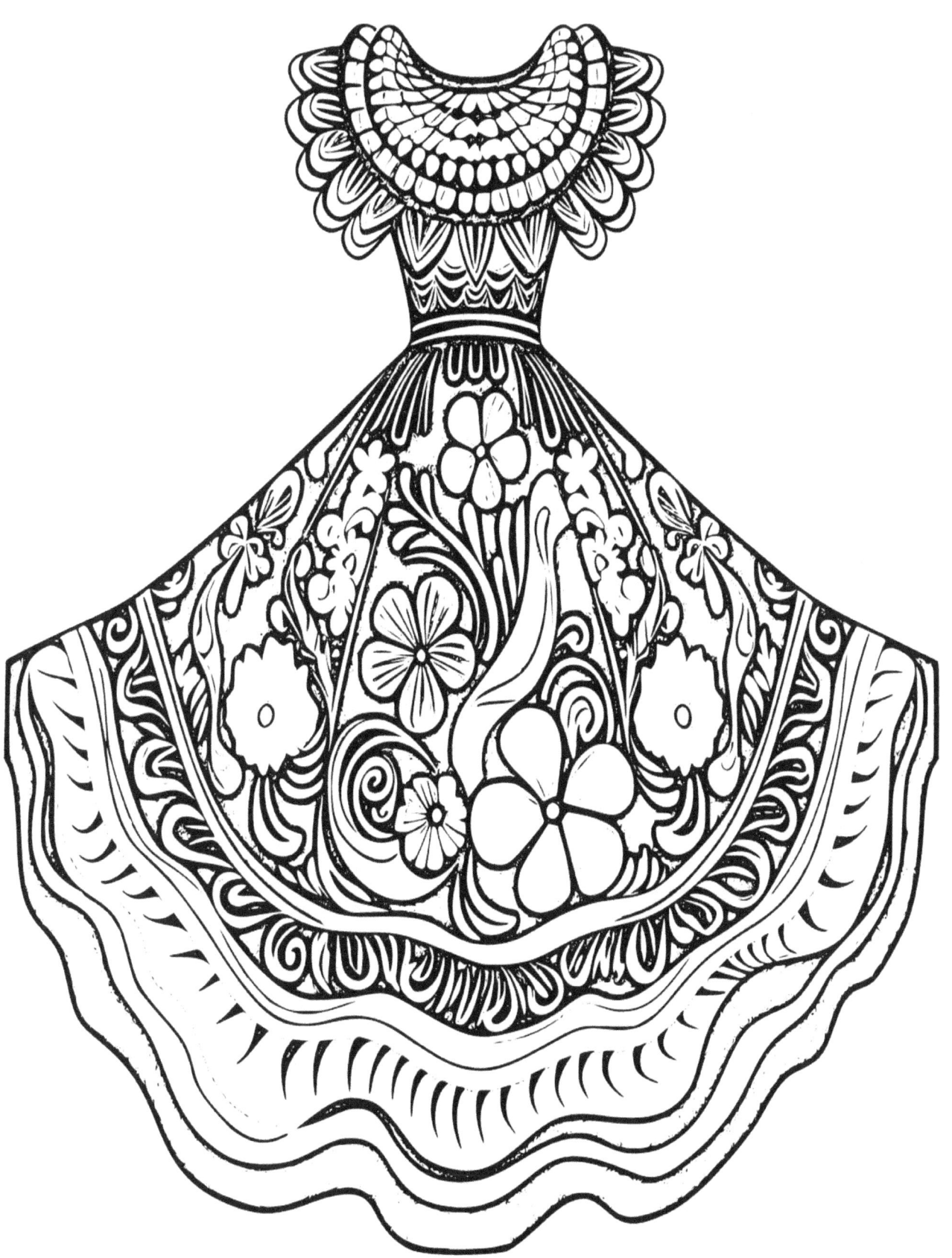

Intentionally Blank
Intencionalmente Blanco

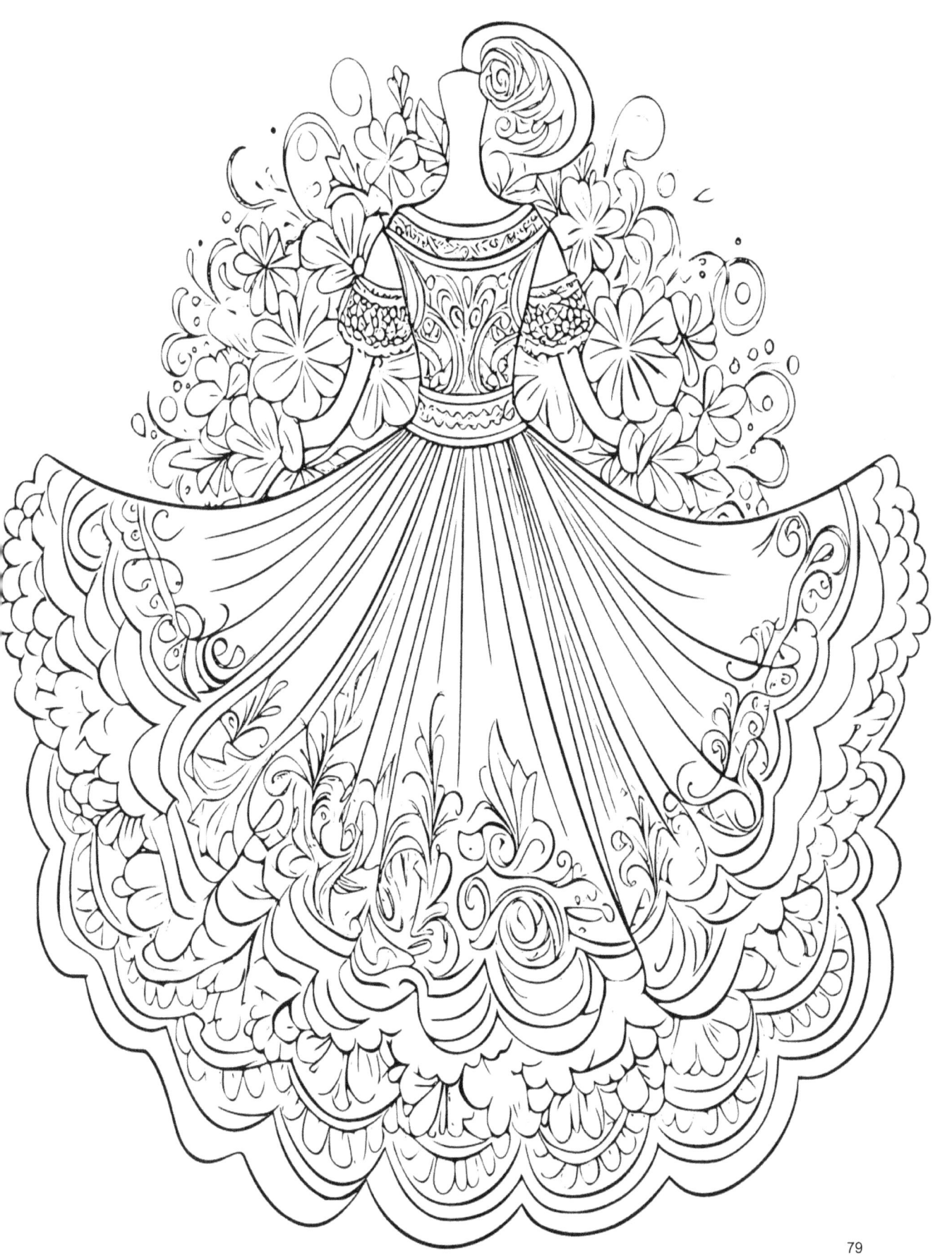

Intentionally Blank
Intencionalmente Blanco

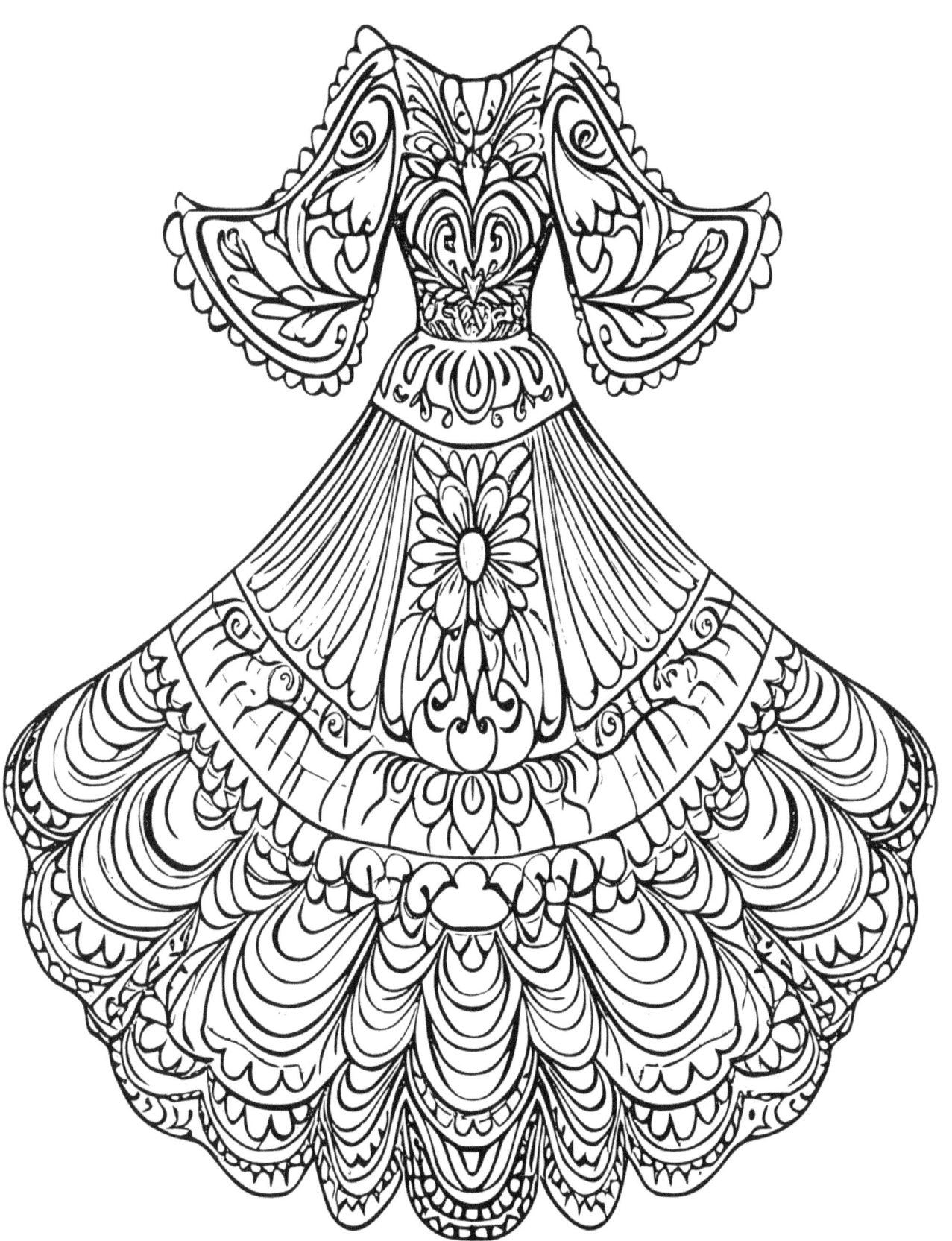

Intentionally Blank
Intencionalmente Blanco

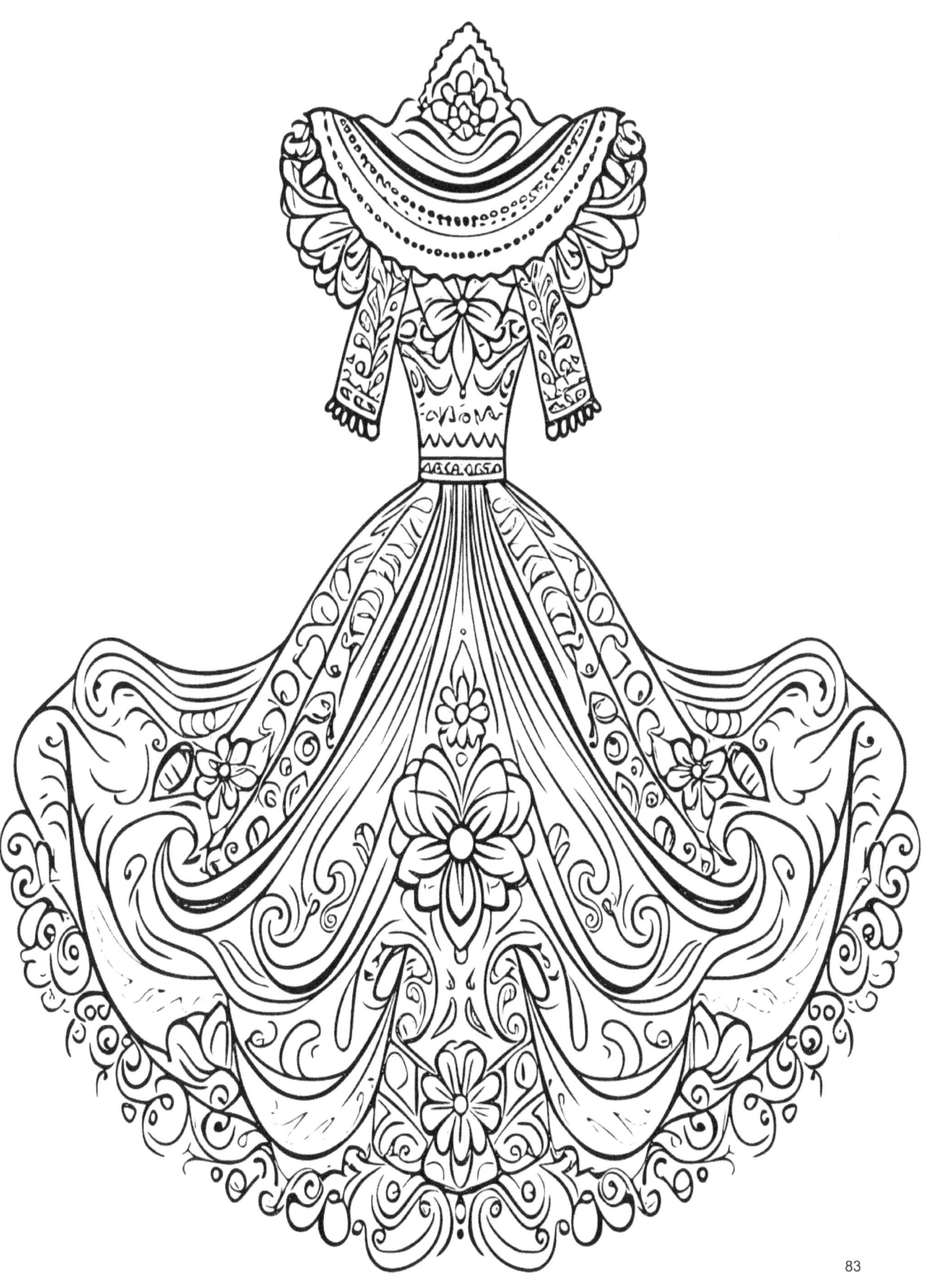

Intentionally Blank
Intencionalmente Blanco

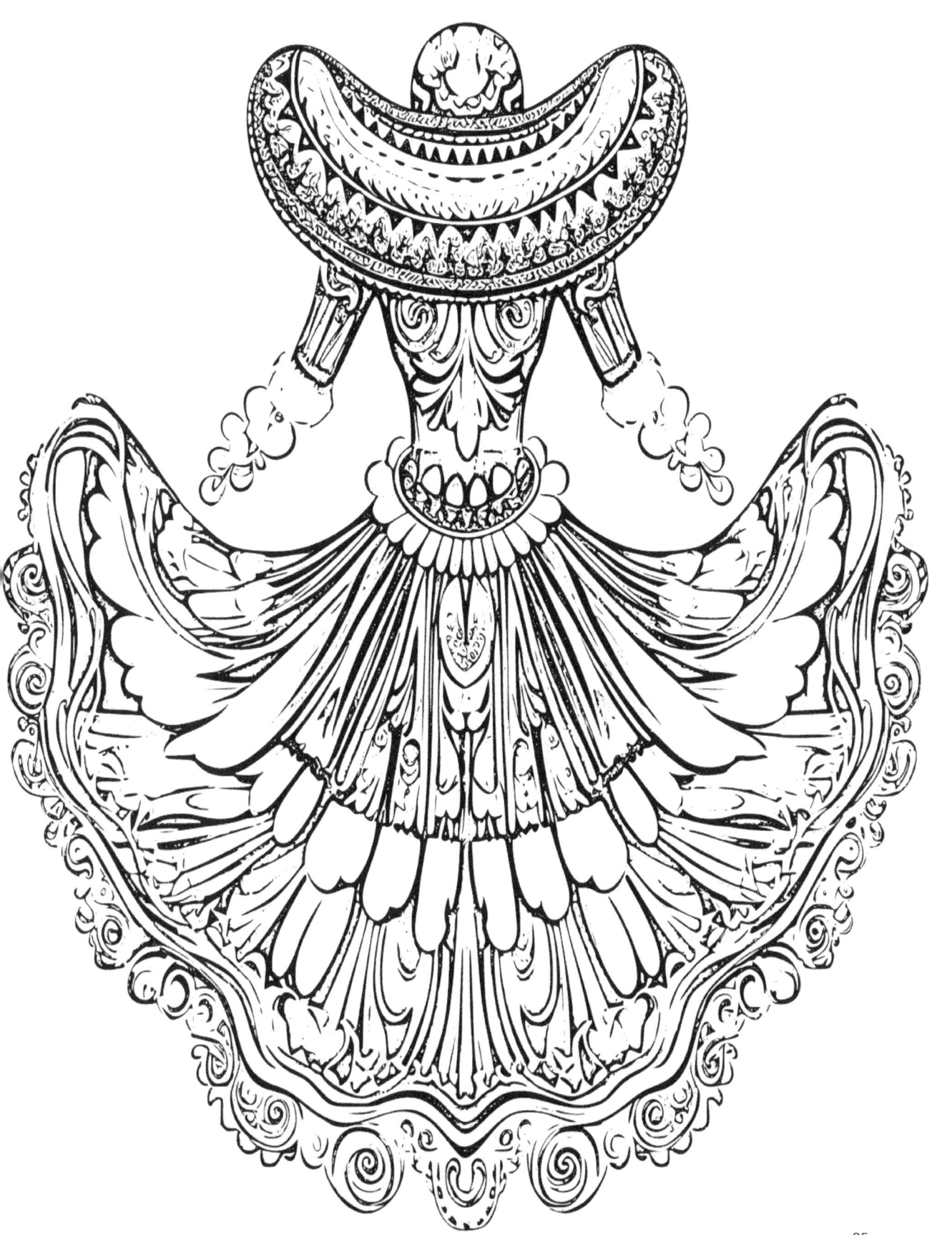

Intentionally Blank
Intencionalmente Blanco

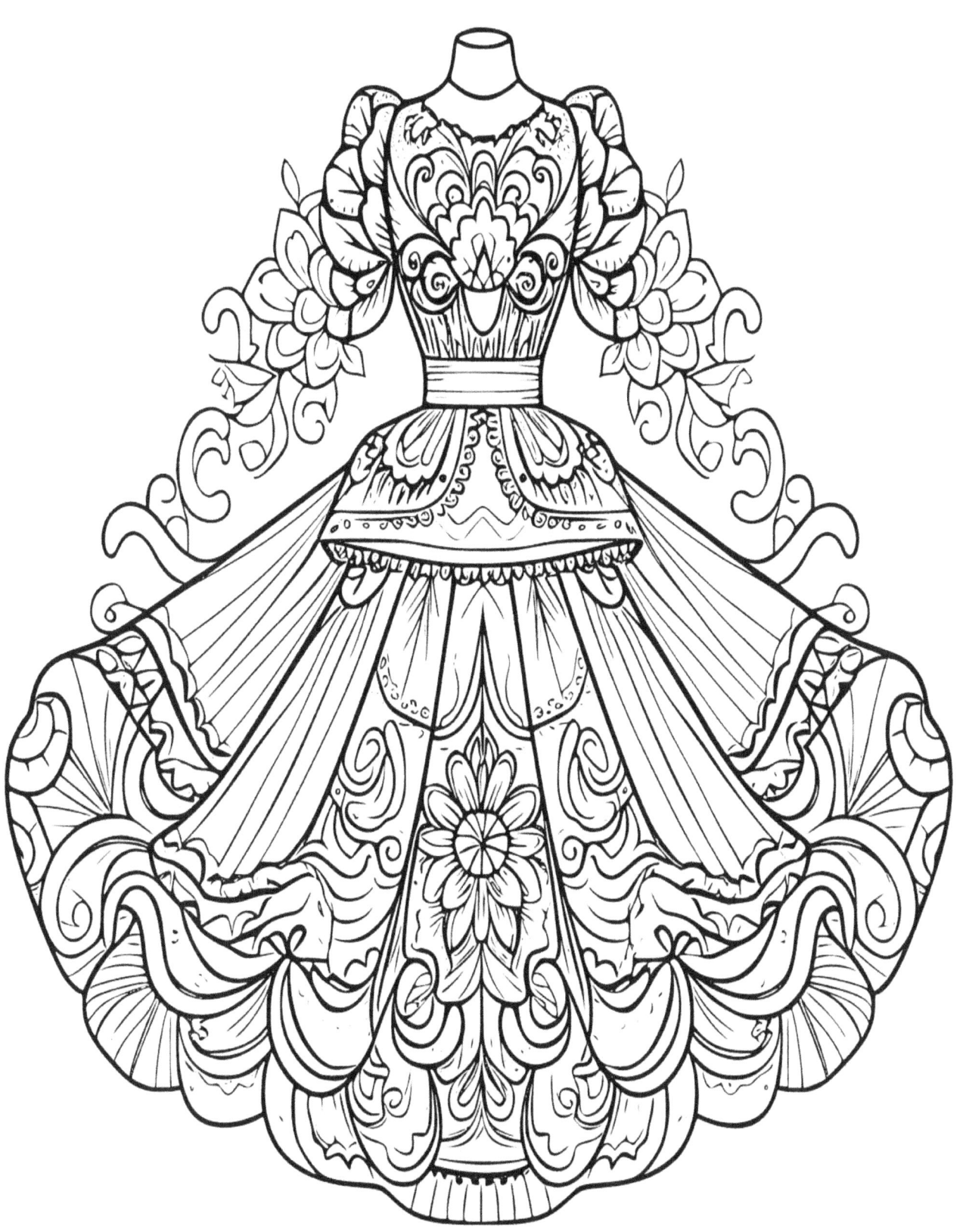

Intentionally Blank
Intencionalmente Blanco

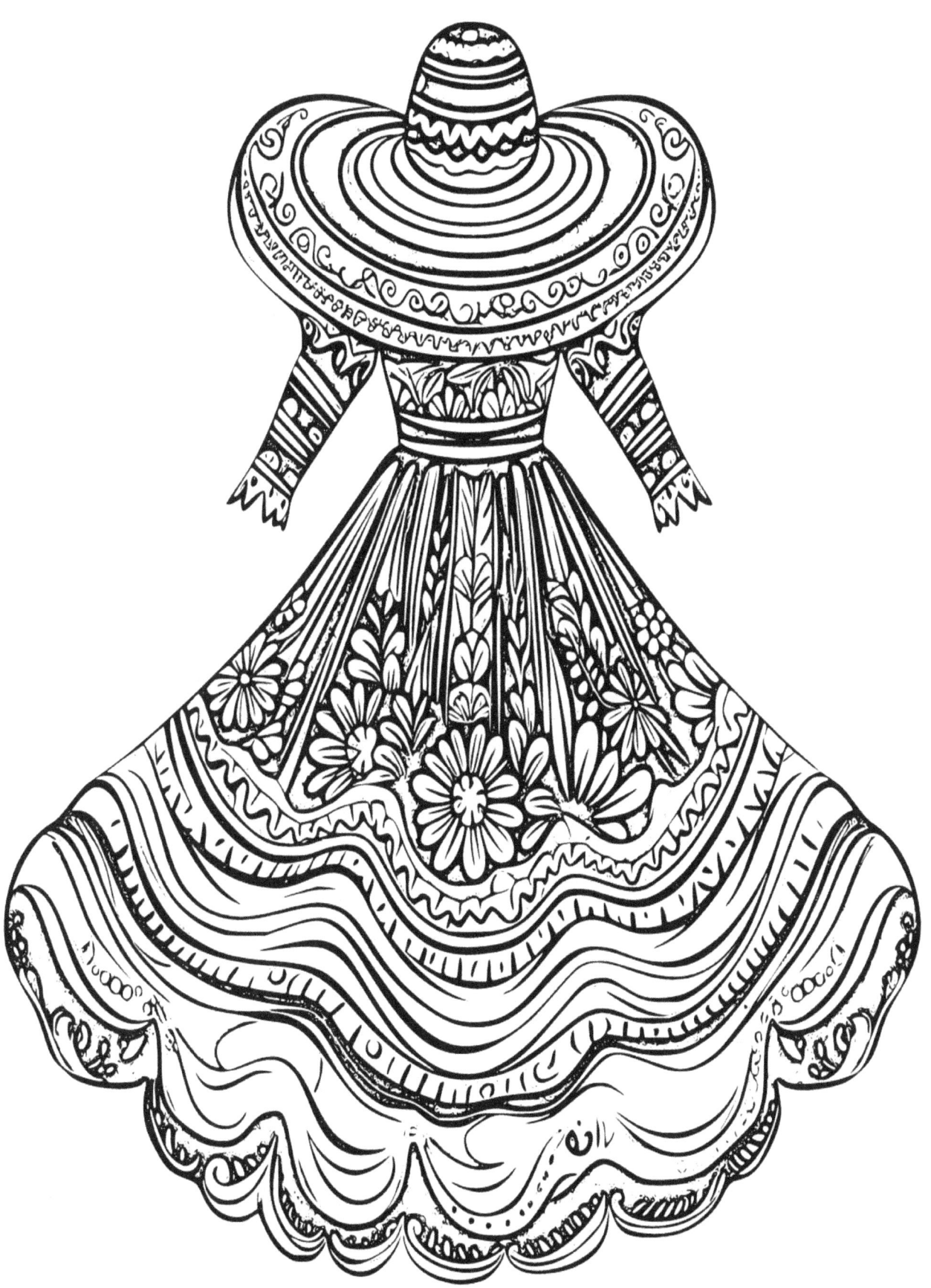

Intentionally Blank
Intencionalmente Blanco

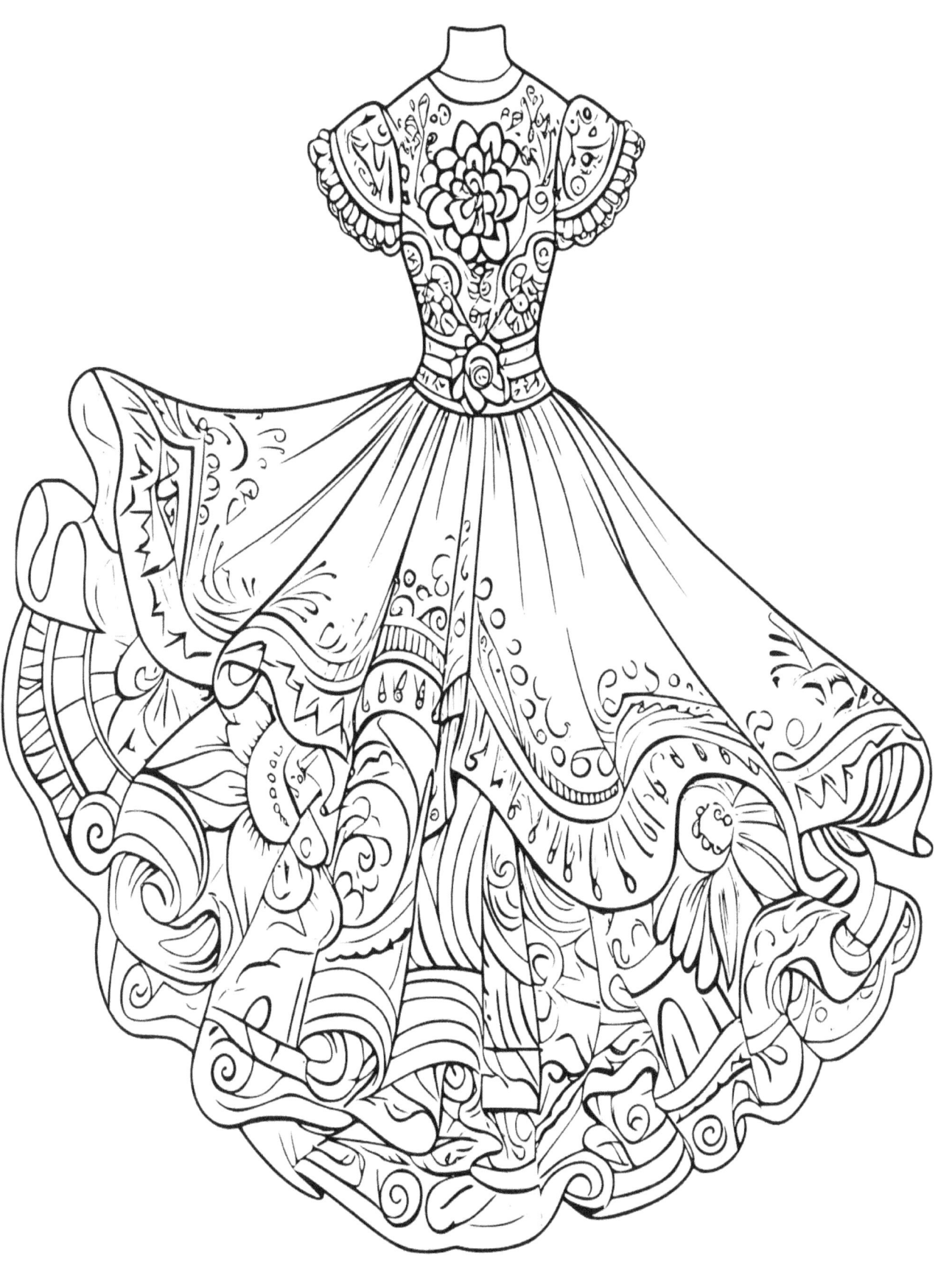

Intentionally Blank
Intencionalmente Blanco

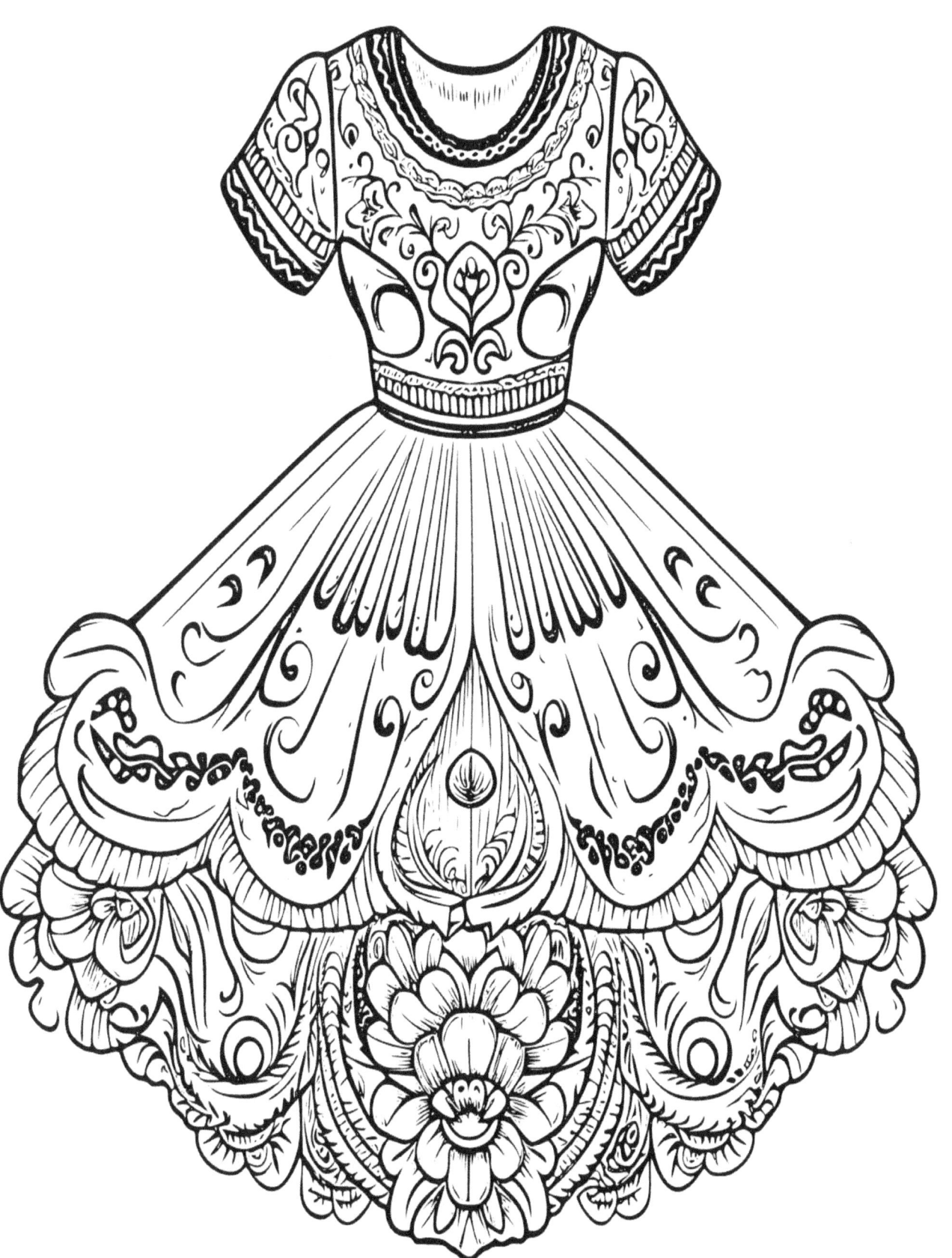

Intentionally Blank
Intencionalmente Blanco

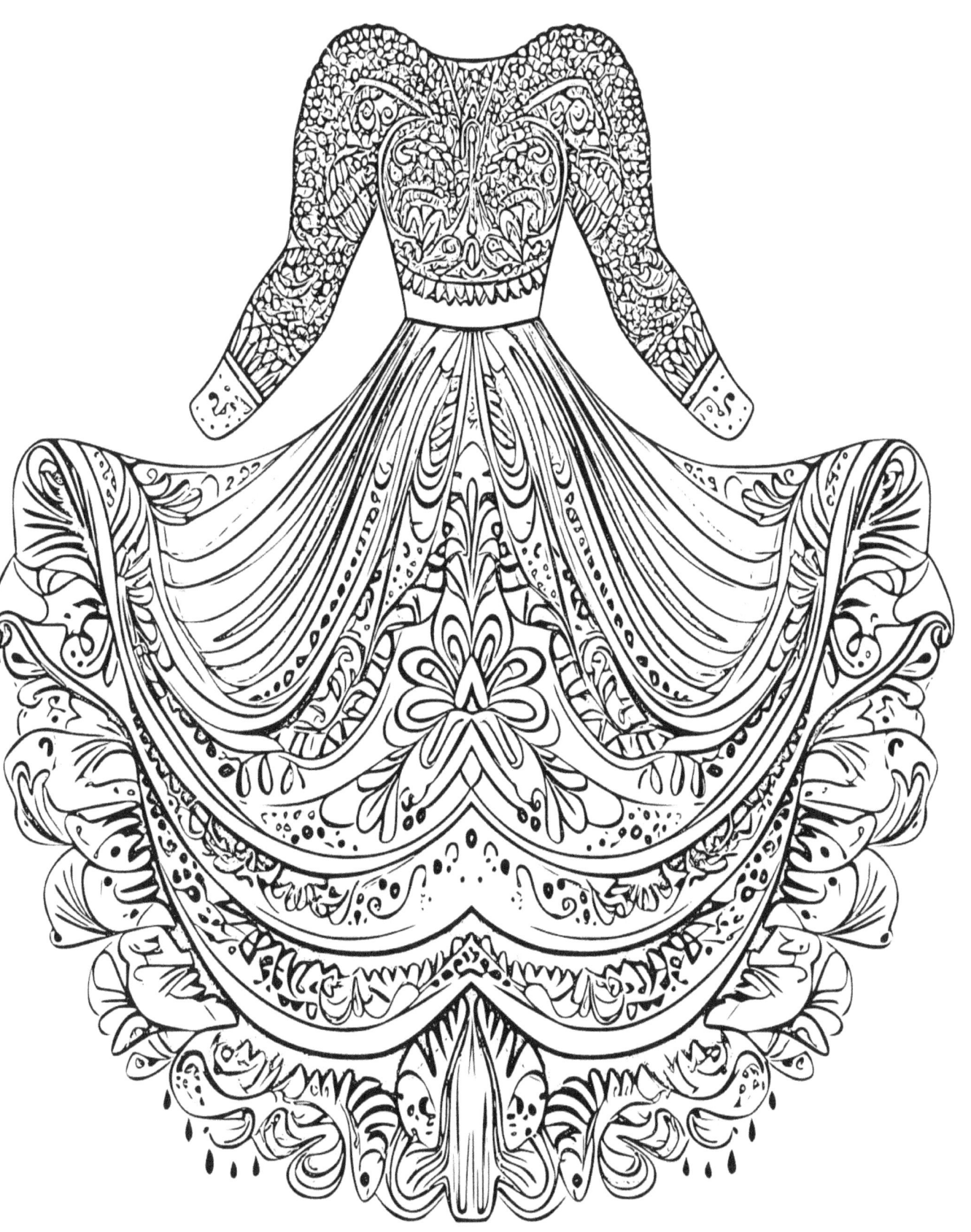

Intentionally Blank
Intencionalmente Blanco

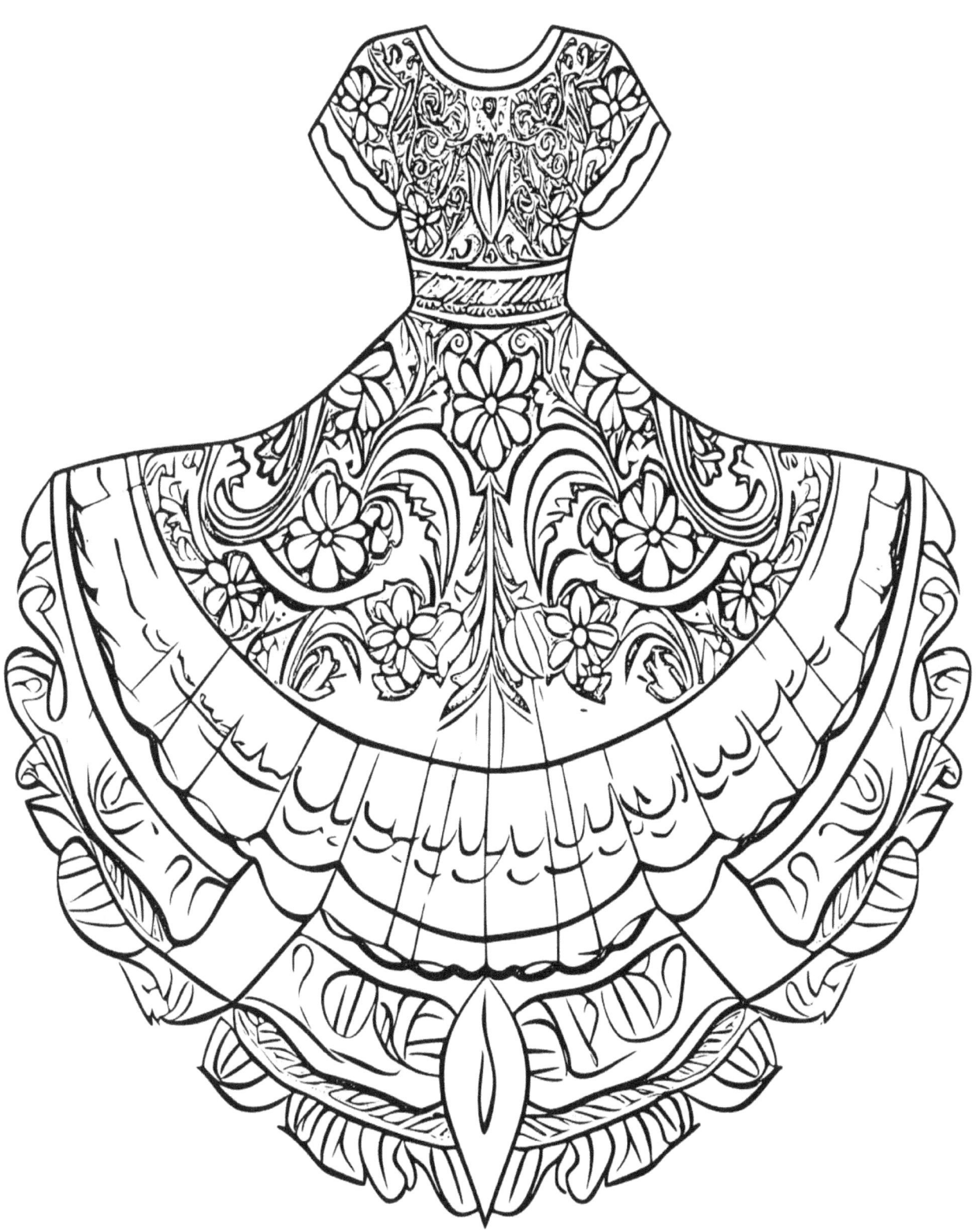

Intentionally Blank
Intencionalmente Blanco

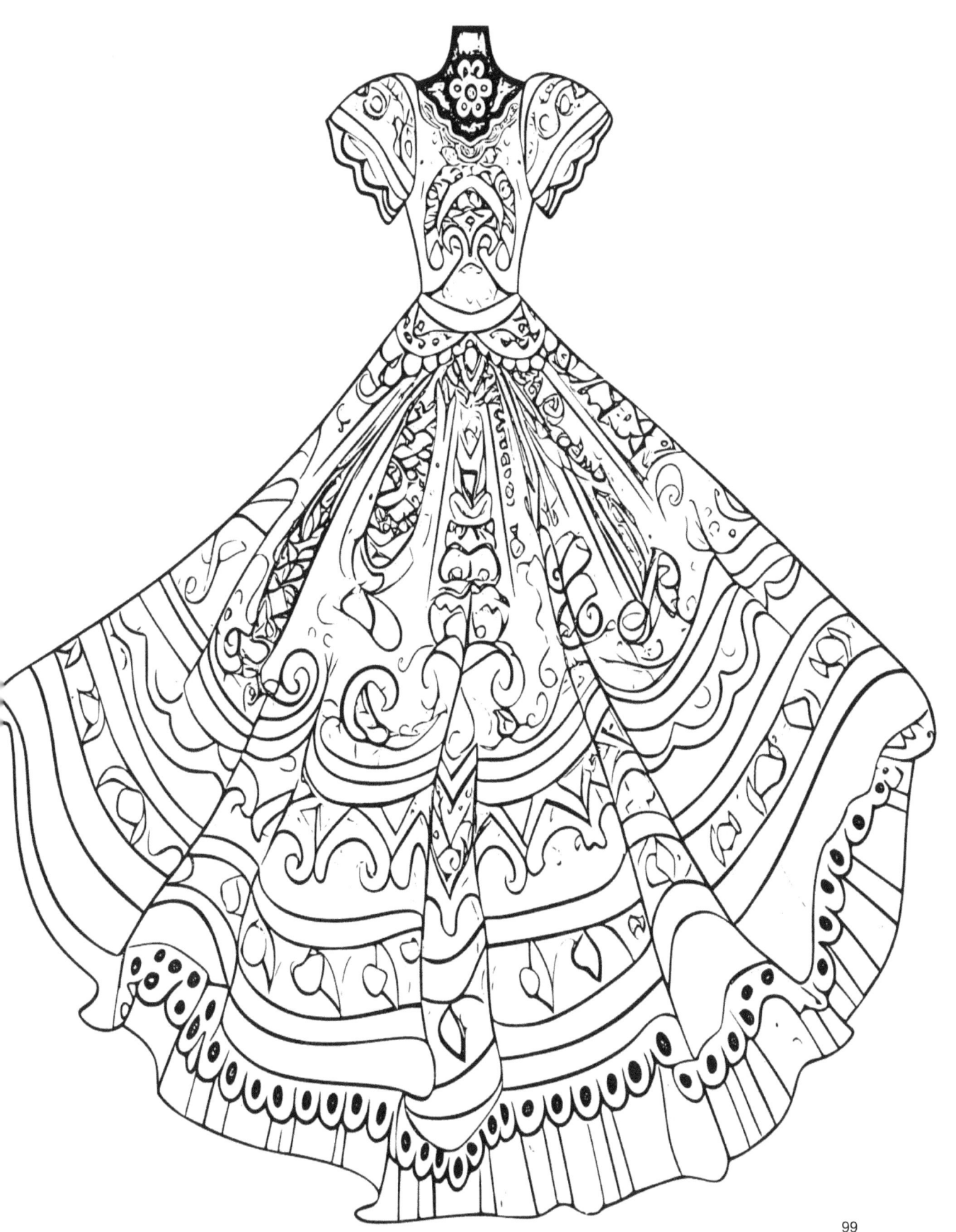

Intentionally Blank
Intencionalmente Blanco

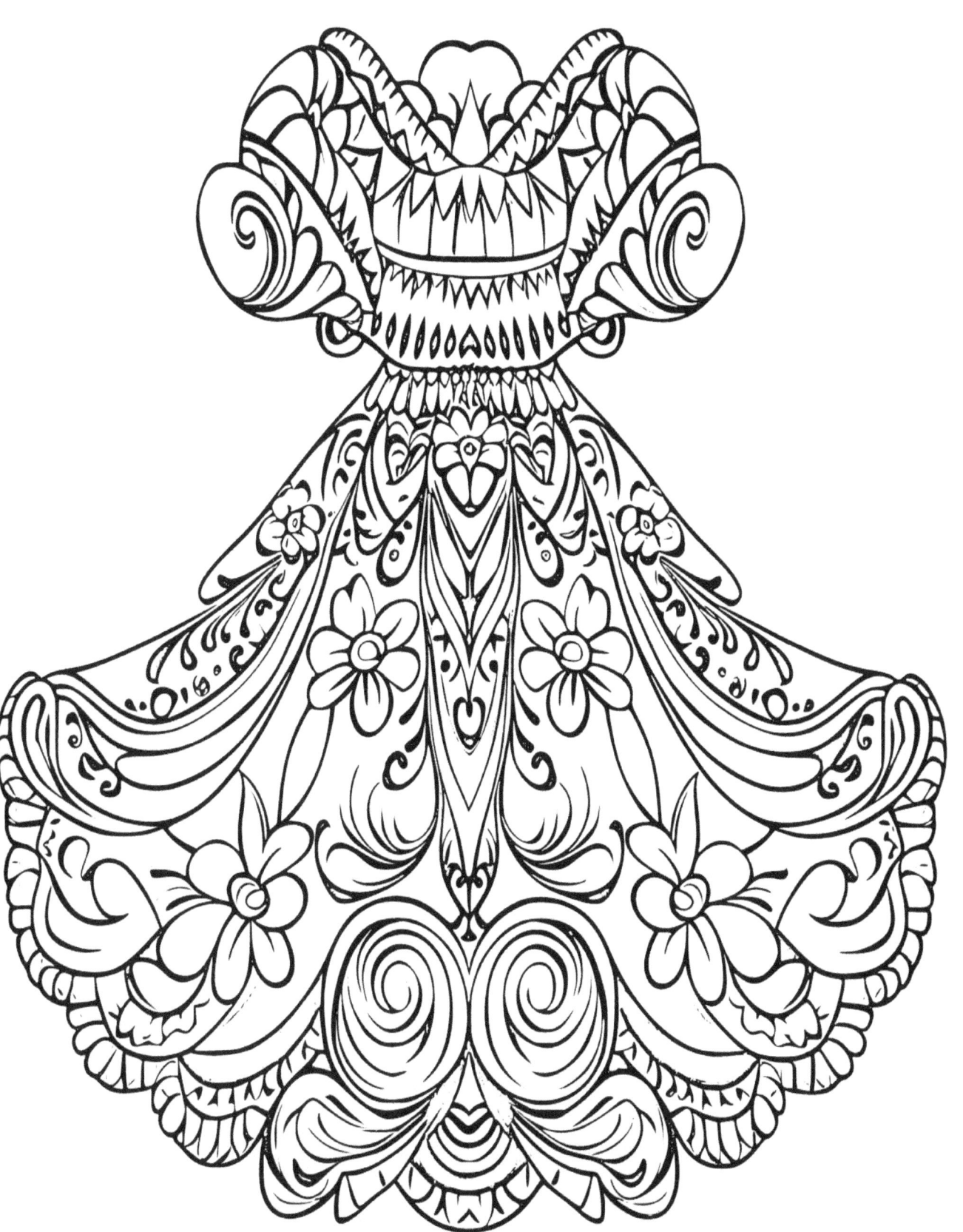

Intentionally Blank
Intencionalmente Blanco

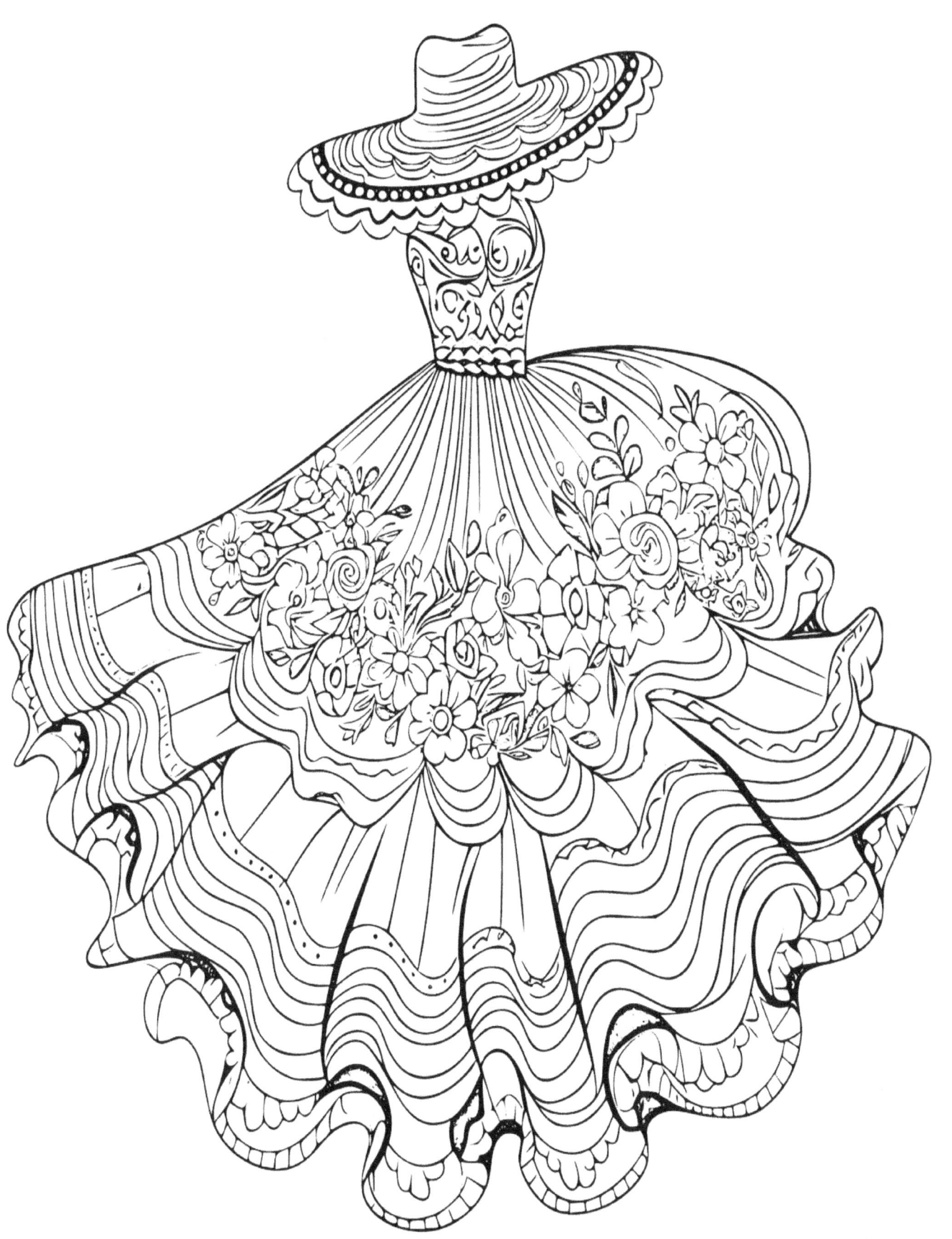

Intentionally Blank
Intencionalmente Blanco

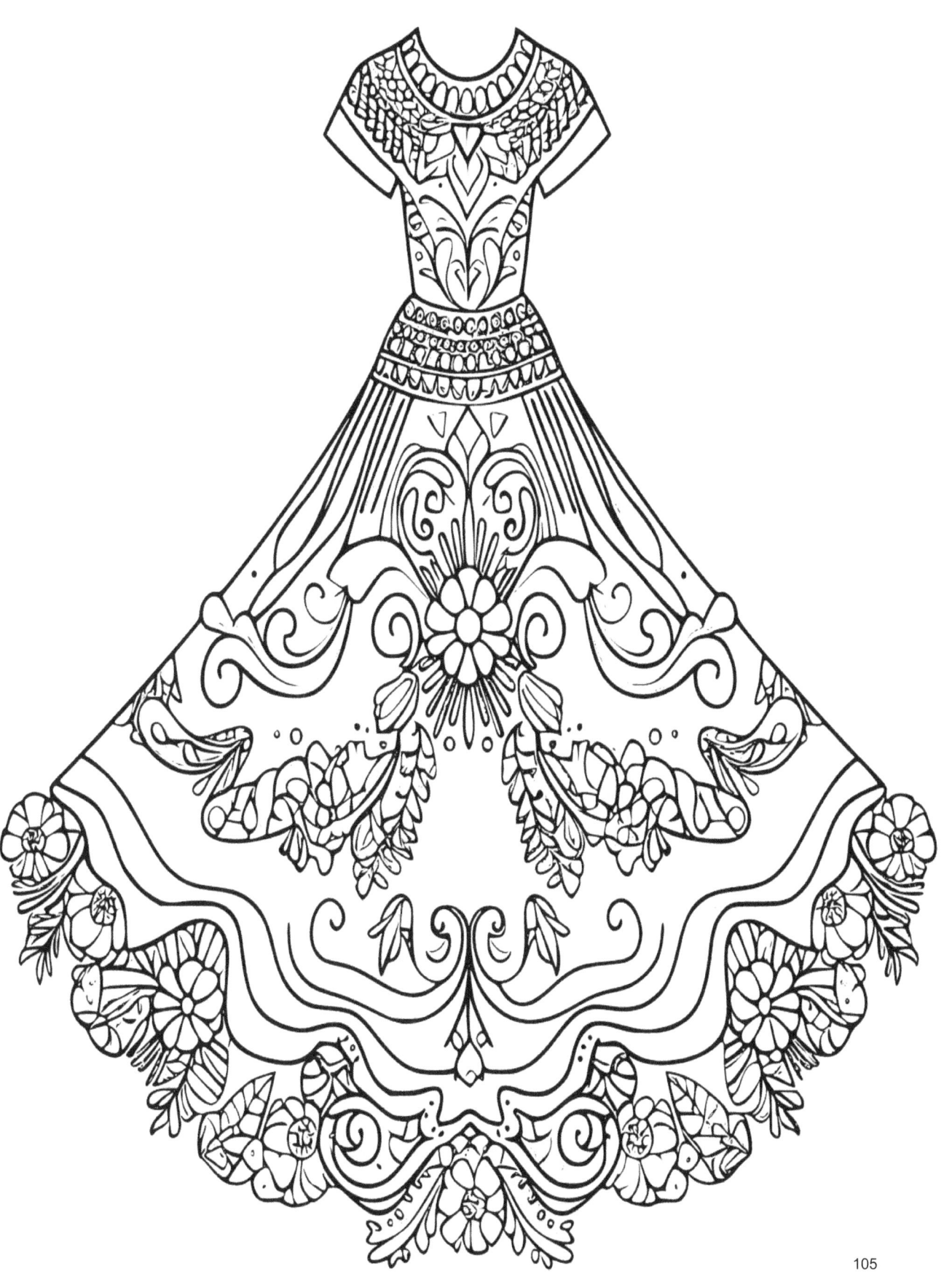

Intentionally Blank
Intencionalmente Blanco

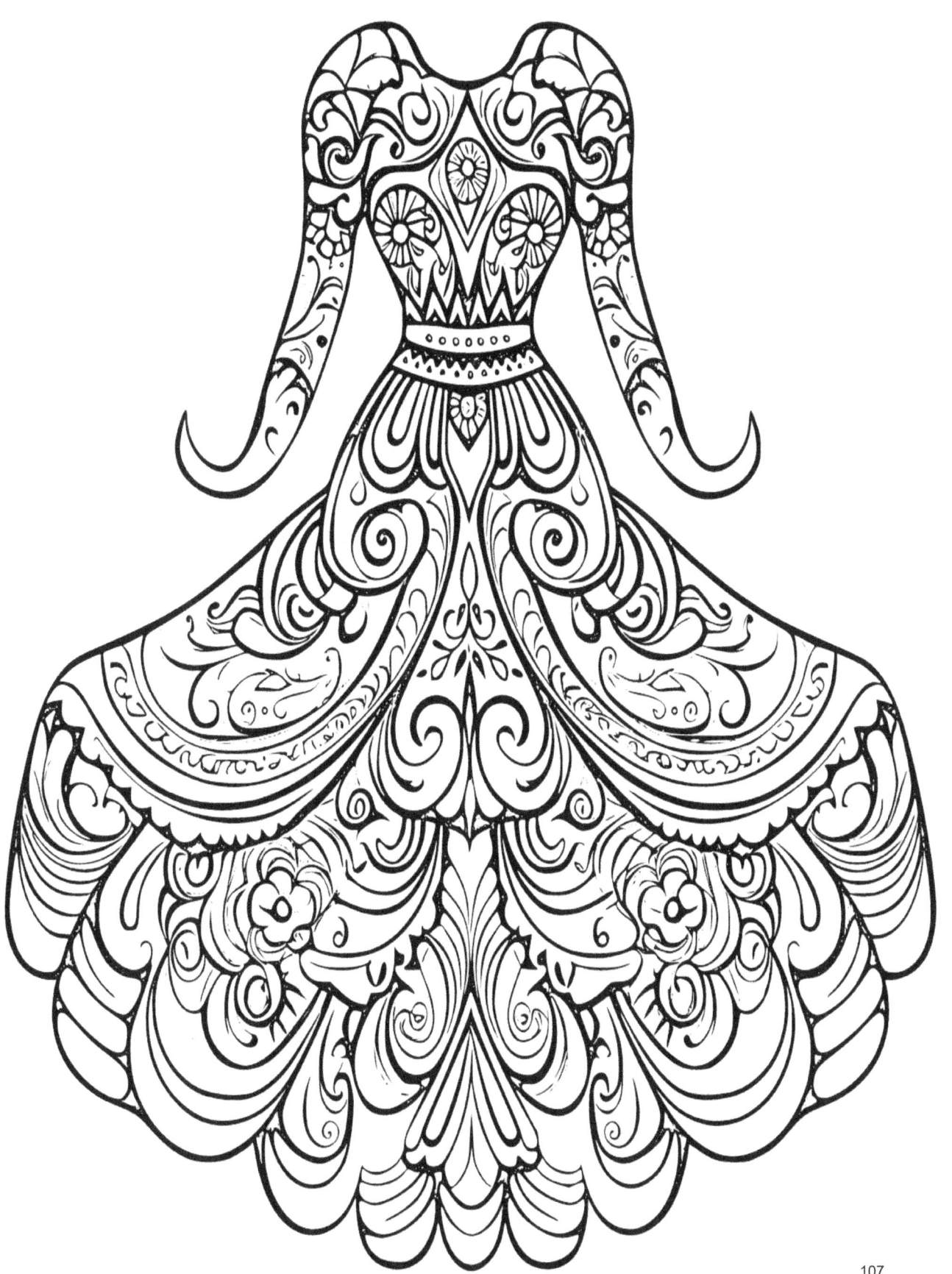

Este libro está dedicado a
Mi Bella Esposa

Thank you so much for making it this far!

I appreciate the time you took to give my book a read. As a small individual publisher, it means a lot, and I hope I am making a difference in your life's journey.

If you have 60 seconds, hearing your honest feedback on Amazon would mean the world to me. It does wonders for the book, and I love hearing about your experience with it.

To leave your feedback:

1. Open your camera app
2. Point your mobile device at the QR code below
3. The review page will appear in your web browser

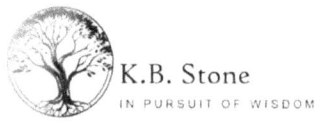